Designing the
NEW KITCHEN GARDEN

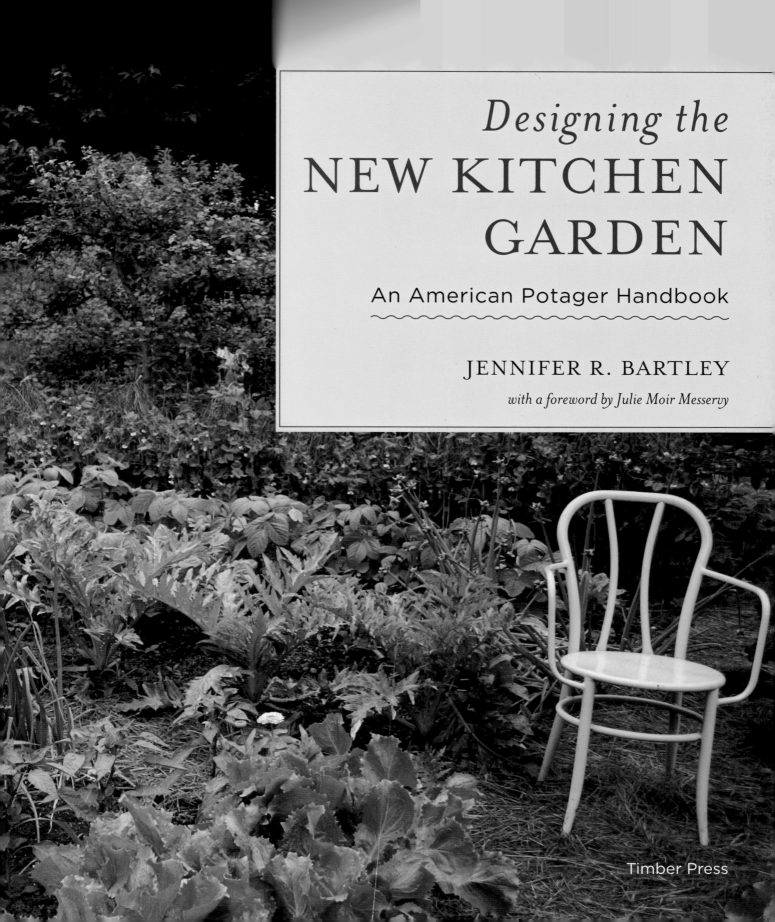

Designing the
NEW KITCHEN
GARDEN

An American Potager Handbook

JENNIFER R. BARTLEY

with a foreword by Julie Moir Messervy

Timber Press

Endpapers: A 15th century enclosed garden, from Crisp 1924.

Title page: The bountiful potager of Wayne Winterrowd and Joe Eck at North Hill in Readsboro, Vermont.

Dedication: Stone steps lined with verbena and blue catmint leading to the kitchen garden of Gay and Tony Barclay in Potomac, Maryland.

Published in 2006 by

Timber Press, Inc.
The Haseltine Building
133 S.W. Second Avenue, Suite 450
Portland, Oregon 97204-3527, U.S.A.
www.timberpress.com

For contact information for editorial, marketing, sales, and distribution in the United Kingdom, see www.timberpress.co/uk.

Printed through Colorcraft Ltd., Hong Kong

Library of Congress Cataloging-in-Publication Data

Bartley, Jennifer R.
  Designing the new kitchen garden : an American potager handbook /
Jennifer R. Bartley ; with a foreword by Julie Moir Messervy.
    p. cm.
  Includes bibliographical references and index.
  ISBN-13: 978-0-88192-772-6
  ISBN-10: 0-88192-772-4
 1. Vegetable gardening. 2. Organic gardening. 3. Kitchen gardens--Design. I. Title.
  SB324.3.B38 2006
  635'.0484--dc22   2006003057

A catalog record for this book is also available from the British Library.

TO RUTH R. MATSON

You always will be an inspiration

BEAUTY WILL SAVE THE WORLD.

Fyodor Dostoyevsky,
The Idiot, 1868

CONTENTS

~~~~~~

~~~~~~

Jennifer R. Bartley's *Designing the New American Kitchen Garden* arrived on my doorstep in the nick of time. My husband and I have just moved into our newly renovated house in Vermont, and now that the contractors have cleared out, I have been dying to finally begin building an edible garden. As a landscape designer and writer for the past thirty years, I know something about building ornamental gardens for people, but it's been literally decades since I last had a vegetable garden: four to be exact!

My last attempt was when I was eleven, the summer that my family moved from Illinois to Connecticut. Not knowing anyone my own age, I had decided to build a huge vegetable garden in a sunny spot surrounded by old apple trees in our new backyard.

I worked so hard. I carefully rototilled and amended the soil, set out string and mounded each row, and sowed in carrots, beans, radishes, melons, pumpkins, lettuce, and tomatoes. I watered, cultivated, thinned, and staked my little plants and just couldn't wait to reap the harvest that would surely come after so much effort on my part. In August, just as the beans were ripe for picking and the young carrots tasted sweet, I left to visit my best friend in our old hometown. Worrying about my garden's upkeep, I cajoled my two younger brothers into harvesting its bounty during my absence.

Two weeks later, when I finally returned home, the first thing I did was run to see how the garden looked. It was gone! Bulldozed down! Without a word, my parents had begun to build a clay tennis court in its place.

Don't worry. I've forgiven my parents. Thanks to them, I'm a respectable tennis player, but still fearful of my ability to build a lasting vegetable garden. That's why Jennifer Bartley's wonderful book is such a gift, not only to me, but to all who are looking to improve their property, their health, and their way of life by creating a space for gardening that includes fruits, vegetables, herbs, and perennials in their own backyard. Jennifer makes a compelling case for creating the American *potager*—a year-round garden that provides the family kitchen with herbs and vegetables on a daily basis, literally filling the family soup pot throughout the four seasons. An experienced gardener and designer herself, she writes evocatively of the tasty delights that come from a kitchen garden and augments her words with thrillingly colorful garden plans and photographs that inspire as well as inform.

Jennifer creates a journey that takes her readers past a series of gastronomic pleasures, researching historical origins of the kitchen garden, walking us through design principles, describing good plant combinations, and explaining how to build and maintain an edible garden. She brings her theory home by following the development of three very different kitchen gardens from around the country, including my friends' Wayne Winterrowd and Joe Eck's wonderful Vermont garden. Jennifer takes us along as she creates gardens for herself, for other homeowners, and for gourmet restaurants, which include outdoor kitchens, outdoor pantries, compost bins, arbors, and her favorite vegetables and herbs.

Throughout the book, Jennifer sprinkles invaluable plant information, including antique rose recommendations, commonly used culinary flowers, and plants that nourish beneficial insects, to name just a few of the resources in this rich volume. Her chart describing when and what to plant where and a list of seed and fruit sources will prove of great practical value to me as I begin my own garden.

Perhaps best of all, Jennifer writes articulately about why edible gardens are so important to our souls. In the section entitled "Restoration Soup," she writes, "Potagers are places of restoration that provide food and nourishment. A deep and mysterious relationship exists between food and having our spirits lifted, and this relationship is profoundly and ultimately tied to the garden." I couldn't agree more.

JULIE MOIR MESSERVY

Julie Moir Messervy is a landscape designer, lecturer, and author of four books, including *The Inward Garden* and, with architect Sarah Susanka, *Outside the Not So Big House: Creating the Landscape of Home*.

PREFACE

~~~~~~

I built a garden, a potager of herbs, flowers, and vegetables, in my own backyard to find a way to move in a positive direction after my mother was diagnosed with Alzheimer's disease. In the midst of her decline, my garden was something to hold on to that wasn't deteriorating.

I returned to school and graduated *summa cum laude* with a degree in landscape architecture from The Ohio State University. I continued to explore lessons in horticulture, urban design, and architecture, receiving the post-professional master's degree in landscape architecture. Much of this book is the result of the thesis work I did to earn that degree.

My childhood summers were spent picking raspberries, blackberries, and elderberries in the fields near our home in central Ohio. My father, brothers, sisters, and I would spend hours on these foraging adventures. It required putting on a long-sleeved shirt and pants, even in July, and finding a handy pail, preferably something with a handle to put over your arm while you picked. So often the berries near the meadow path were small or had already been picked. The biggest and darkest black raspberries were through the brambles. We had to forge our own path to the produce and endure the scratches now and the poison ivy later just to fill the bucket part way. Probably countless berries spilled out of our small hands. We ate most of them before they went into the bucket or on the journey home. The final reward was when my mother transformed the hand-picked precious treasure into a cobbler or pie to savor as the late-afternoon meal.

Black raspberry season was followed by blackberry season, with much bigger but less flavorful berries; then came the elderberries. The small, shiny, black berries were taken off their stems and put in a pot to boil. The juice was poured through a sieve to extract only the dark purple liquid. Sugar and pectin were added and the hot syrup poured into jars and sealed with paraffin. Late in the summer came paw paw season. My father and I gathered the greenish yellow fruit from the native trees growing in the ravine on our property. I remember tasting the homemade wine.

These are some of my favorite childhood memories. Those days have disappeared, because in many communities, farmers' fields are now housing developments, and we don't have the time to spend a summer day picking berries and then making them into a pie. I am afraid our own lives are diminished a bit when we don't take time to eat food that we have gathered or grown and prepared. How do we now create memories for our children?

As a designer, I draw on many aspects to develop my designs, including history and historical gardens. But my interest in the walled garden is an interest in architecture and the knowledge that our surroundings have a profound effect on us. Gardens heal us not just because of the physical labor of planting and weeding and harvesting, although this connection to nature and the seasons is profound, but because of the sensual physicality of the plants and the walls—the beautiful space itself that transforms our minds. My hope is that you will be inspired to build your own potager and discover the healing power of a beautiful edible garden, and that you will begin to grow your own food to enjoy with those you love.

Bon jardinage.
Bon appétit.

ACKNOWLEDGMENTS

Many people have contributed to this book. First of all, I must thank the owners of the public and private gardens who allowed me to visit and photograph them. You are so generous in sharing your special places: Henri Carvallo from Château de Villandry; Patrice Taravella and Sonia Lesot from Prieuré d'Orsan; Hubert Mourot from Jardin Médiéval de Bois Richeux; Muriel de Curel from Saint-Jean de Beauregard; and Manuel Pluvinage, director at the École Nationale Superieure du Paysage, which manages Le Potager du Roi.

I owe an immense thanks to Mike Shoup, owner of the Antique Rose Emporium; Wayne Winterrowd and Joe Eck at North Hill; Gay Barclay and her garden; Sandy Clinton at Clinton and Associates; Chip Shepherd and chef Craig Shelton at The Ryland Inn; Magdiale Wolmark and Cristin Austin at Dragonfly Neo-V Cuisine; Corrine Yager and her garden; Holly Watson and her garden; and Dorsey Barger and Elaine Martin at East Side Café. I have enjoyed talking with and learning from each of you. Your gardens and restaurants are an important part of this book. Thank you to Tom Fischer and Eve Goodman and everyone at Timber Press for your kindness, support, and hard work in this venture. Thank you to my editor, Lisa Theobald, for her input and clear way of seeing and communicating.

Dr. Martin F. Quigley, I would have never started this project without your nudging; you grasped the potential of this work early on. Thank you. My family has been a huge support, especially my husband, Terry Bartley, for which I am deeply grateful. Thank you to my five children, Katie, Matt, John, Jim, and Travis, who sacrificed their mother and home to the huge task of illustrating, writing, and creating—a sometimes messy process. My sister, Sally Schmitt, took the trip to France with me that began this adventure. Sally and my father, James E. Matson, also were my traveling companions to New Jersey and Vermont. You and other family members have helped in so many ways—thank you. My son John and Sara Rimelspach helped immensely with my own garden. Thanks to friends Mark and Kristen Hagen in Texas and George and Beth Sebek in Maryland for your hospitality. Thank you to Mike Lonchar, Holly Watson, Judy Steckel, and Gail Walls for endless encouragement and support.

Freshly picked golden scallopini bush squash from the Watson potager will be sautéed in extra virgin olive oil with freshly grated parmesan cheese added on top.

CHAPTER ONE

Origins

WHAT IS A POTAGER? Translated literally from French, *potage* means a soup of broth with vegetables. For Europeans, *le potager* has come to mean simply a vegetable garden (*jardin des légumes*). But the term *potager* carries with it a much deeper historical tradition. This meaning stretches back to the Middle Ages when all of Western civilization—literature, history, and science—was hanging by a slender thread, hidden behind the high stone walls of medieval monasteries. These cultural outposts were small, isolated, and largely self-sufficient. For the most part, the monks and nuns grew their own food, herbs, and medicines. Within small geometric plots, useful herbs, vegetables, and perhaps some flowers for the chapel altar were grown year-round for daily use. Monastery gardens were more than vegetable gardens, however; they were also used as sites for meditation and prayer.

JUST A KITCHEN GARDEN?

Georgeanne Brennan, cookbook author and owner of a cooking school in Provence, describes a potager as a year-round kitchen garden whose purpose is to supply the kitchen with fresh vegetables and herbs on a daily basis. The French have always grasped this important connection between the garden and the kitchen. The nearby potager supplies food for the household, and what is grown in the garden is served at the table.

The term *jardin potager* first appeared in 1567 in the Charles Estienne and Jean Liébault work *L'Agriculture et Maison Rustique*, in reference to a garden of edible plants. Later, the word *potager* was used on its own to mean the same thing. A potager is different from the traditional American kitchen garden, which is typically planted in the spring and harvested in the fall, with all surplus being canned, dried, or otherwise preserved for the winter months. In former generations in America, the majority of citizens were farmers. In addition to whatever cash crop they produced, rural families depended on their own gardens for fresh and preserved foods. These gardens were not designed in the sense of an ornamental garden: farm wives had large plots fenced against roaming domestic animals, and these gardens, even with a few flowers, were entirely utilitarian. The gardens were laid out much like smaller versions of the plowed fields in the landscapes around them.

In their Summer 2001 catalog, Ellen Ecker Ogden and Shepherd Ogden, authors and cofounders of The Cook's Garden in Warminster, Pennsylvania, wrote:

> The new American kitchen garden is a place where gardening is a pleasure for both the gardener and the cook, a place to grow both vegetables and flowers together for the simple delight of watching them blossom and fruit, and the pure pleasures they provide the table. Our own kitchen garden is the center of our summer months, and we spend as much time there as possible because tending it is a pleasure, not a chore.

The definition of a traditional kitchen garden depicts a seasonally used space defined separately from the rest of the residential garden—the ornamental plants and lawn areas. And, in fact, most suburban vegetable gardens are still miniature versions of grandmother's farm plot. They are rectangular areas consisting of regular, mounded, mulched rows: one row of beans, one row of tomatoes, and one row of squash—more than the family will consume. Annual flowers may be in another bed or border, and shrubs and blooming perennials are on the other side of the house, where the neighbors can see them. These traditional kitchen gardens are not designed, and we tend to apologize for their lack of aesthetic appeal by sticking them in the far reaches of the backyard, out of sight.

What makes the potager different from a typical vegetable garden is not just its history, but its design: the potager is a landscape feature that does not have to be hidden in the corner of the backyard, but can be the central feature of an ornamental, all-season landscape—even in the front yard of a home in the most exclusive residential neighborhood. The potager is a source of herbs, vegetables, and flowers, but it is also a structured garden space, a design based on repetitive geometric patterns.

While the typical vegetable garden is a bare rectangle of soil and mulch throughout the dormant season, the beauty of the potager is that it has year-round visual appeal and can incorporate permanent perennial or woody plantings around (or among) the annual plants. Evergreen shrubs are planted with perennial roses and annual vegetables. Thus, the potager is more than a vegetable plot: it becomes an outdoor room, with "carpet" and "furniture." It can be near the kitchen door in a suburban yard, or it can be the central design in an urban garden. It is a well-designed place that feeds the soul as well as the stomach. It can be tiny—four small squares and just a few species of plants—or opulent and bursting with color, texture, scent, shape, and exuberant placement of the plants. The potager is a simple concept that enables any of us with a garden, small or large, to design for year-round visual satisfaction, while reaping the bounty of the edible and fragrant fruits, vegetables, and flowers it provides.

A raised bed with wattle fencing, as used in medieval gardens, at the Musée National du Moyen Age, Paris.

The potager is more than a simple kitchen garden; it is a philosophy of living in harmony with nature. It is a dependence on the seasons and the earth to supply the bounty of flavors and textures for the kitchen; in the spring we enjoy a salad of red radicchio with white radishes and early peas, a dessert of strawberries and cream with a sprinkle of candied violets, and for the table vase a bouquet of fragrant heirloom peonies. In the height of the summer, a quick sauce of coarsely chopped tomatoes, basil, Italian parsley, onions, and garlic is served over pasta; the green beans never make it to the table, as they are eaten sweet and raw from the vine, while the tomatoes, herbs, and flowers are gathered into a basket. Some lavender blossoms are folded into a vanilla custard for desert, while additional purple stems are gathered along with the chartreuse flowers of 'Envy' zinnias (*Zinnia elegans* 'Envy') for the table decoration. The light begins to change in the season of harvest (although we have been harvesting and replanting all summer—not just once in the autumn). The flavors become deeper and richer—a spicy pumpkin soup is cooked within the fleshy shell. The brown remnants of the late fall garden, when frost has killed the sensitive heat-loving vegetables, remind us that if fate is kind to us, we can do it all again next year, season by season, and then again the year after that. Before the garden is cleared and prepared for the winter, we gather a few seeds from a favorite calendula and heirloom tomato. This becomes

Teaching our children about food, its origins, growth, taste, and freshness begins in the garden. Without stepping on the freshly planted border of lavender, my nieces Kristen and Laura pick leaves from a spring mix of red, green, and speckled lettuces in my potager.

the hope for the next spring season and ensures that we pass on these memories and flavors to our children.

The potager carries with it a counterpoint and irony of meanings. It is a designed garden with the gardener controlling and dominating the landscape, yet it is a respectful concession to time, the circular rotation of the seasons, and the power of nature. The potager is a paradox of control and intervention and patience and acceptance. It is a reminder of our humble state to plant a dry, brown seed into fertile soil and watch it grow, without any assistance, into a fragrant and colorful vine producing bright green dangling pods or a plant with pungent, tiny, softly hairy leaves to walk on with bare feet. It is always a miracle when we scatter a few seeds in various locations in the bare spring earth, and then with patient anticipation, by the end of the summer, we are engulfed by a garden of fragrant, edible, useful, and beautiful plants. The potager garden is a beautifully designed garden room where we grow the flowers, fruits, herbs, and vegetables we use in the home.

The enclosed garden is a haven of beauty. A modern version of *hortus conclusus*, an enclosed garden of the soul, is very much needed as a model of design for our busy, cluttered lives. We need a garden where we can escape the stresses of urban life, a designed space to step into to forget about traffic, work, and deadlines. We can create an oasis where every sense is brought back to its fullness. This is the modern potager garden—a garden of any size—that fits into our urban or suburban worlds, where we can find healing restoration for our souls and unique specialty delights for our stomachs. Gardens revive us. The very act of tilling, planting, harvesting, and then preparing food strengthens and deeply satisfies us. It is even more rewarding when this garden is part of our homes, where we can enjoy its spiritual and physical bounty every day.

THE EARLIEST KITCHEN GARDENS

We need to understand historical gardens, not to re-create an authentic monastic or medieval garden, but to apply the literal design model of the medieval *hortus conclusus* and a bit of the simple, balanced agrarian lifestyle that is healing and dependent on fresh, authentic food. It reminds us of the possibilities of balancing spirit, soul, and body. It helps us think about our homes and gardens as bits of paradise, where friends and family can

Garden with wattle fence, 1435. (Crisp 1924)

A 15th century enclosed garden with flowing water, flowers, wattle fence, and pear tree. (Crisp 1924)

come to be refreshed and healed, and our potager gardens as workshops, where we hone the art of growing and preserving edible delights. This is the lesson for modern living—that our gardens would be a source of pleasure and healing to those that visit us.

Paradise gardens

In Western Europe, the form of the traditional kitchen garden—four quadrants with a water source in the center—evolved from a combination of symbolism and the local environment of the gardens of Egypt, Persia, Mesopotamia, and Babylon. The early Persian gardens were walled gardens that contained shady, green vegetation and canals of flowing water; this was a direct contrast to the surrounding harsh, brown desert climate. The tree, so rare in the desert, became a symbol of life and fertility. The Persian kings used these enclosed gardens as royal game parks, where they could hunt for exercise and recreation. The gardens were lush and contained fragrant fruit trees, under which one could relax and indulge in sweet refreshment with the cooling sounds of precious bubbling water. Date, fig, and pomegranate trees supplied life-giving sustenance.

This is the origin of our word *paradise*, which comes from the Persian *pairidaeza* and literally means a wall enclosing a garden or an orchard. Later, visiting Greeks were so enamored of these lush gardens that they adopted the word *paradeisos*, which is translated as park, garden, or pleasure ground. In Greek translations of the Bible, *paradeisos* was used for the Garden of Eden. The idea of paradise as a heavenly abode became interchangeable with the Garden of Eden, and it was understood that the garden was enclosed.

Roman gardens

An architectural feature derived first from the Greeks and then the Romans, the *peristyle* is a colonnade surrounding a garden open to the sky. Typically it was in the center of the dwelling with rooms arranged around it. This central garden was the foundation of Roman family life, where they entertained, rested, and placed representations of their deities. The rooms of the house were shut off from the street, and views were directed inward through the covered columns into the garden. This open central garden created a special haven of light and breezes to cool the house. The garden was lush with edible plants and pools of water, creating a private paradise for the owner, the size and lavish quality limited only by the owner's means. Later the peristyle—with its layers of central open garden, covered walkway, and internal rooms—was adapted to Islamic gardens and to the cloister in monastic gardens.

Islamic gardens

Islamic gardens embraced the concept of representing paradise on earth through the enclosed garden. These gardens also contained linear canals of water that represented the rivers flowing from the Garden of Eden, dividing the garden into four quadrants.

Genesis 2:8–10, from the King James Version, describes the first garden:

> And the Lord God planted a garden eastward in Eden; and there he put the man whom he had formed.
> And out of the ground made the Lord God to grow every tree that is pleasant to the sight, and good for food; the tree of life also in the midst of the garden, and the tree of knowledge of good and evil.
> And a river went out of Eden to water the garden; and from thence it was parted, and became into four heads.

This was the goal of the earliest kitchen gardens, in both the Muslim and Judeo-Christian tradition: to get back to the original, perfect garden where humankind was at peace with God and nature. Create a lush, green garden with fruit trees like the Tree of Life, producing every kind of fruit. Create a garden where the most beautiful flora growing in perfect harmony would surround the visitor with fragrant, cooling textures of green with highlights of every imaginable hue to please the eye and the tongue. This was a reminder of heaven, where all manner of delights would be enjoyed in a garden of shade and flowing water for the faithful believer.

Two archetypes: East and West

Two archetypes developed from this obsession with Eden. Both were inspired by the surrounding landscape. The Eastern archetype is the oasis in the desert. The cooling shade of trees and running water provide a refuge for the weary traveler. This concept of safety was transferred later to the Western archetype as the clearing in the wilderness.

The Eastern archetype of the oasis.

The landscape of Western Europe was entirely different from the desert. In many places, temperate forest covered the land. In the Middle Ages, an opening in the dense, sometimes unknown and unsafe forest, was a refuge. The Eastern and Western traditions both have the same meaning, that of a haven and refuge, a place of protection and a representation of heaven on earth. This is the foundation of the *hortus conclusus*.

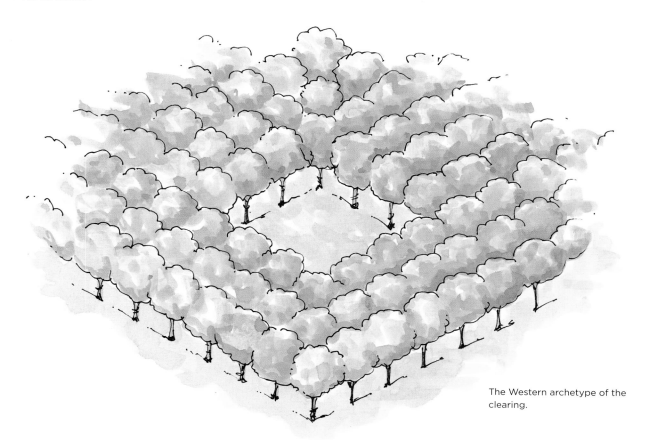

The Western archetype of the clearing.

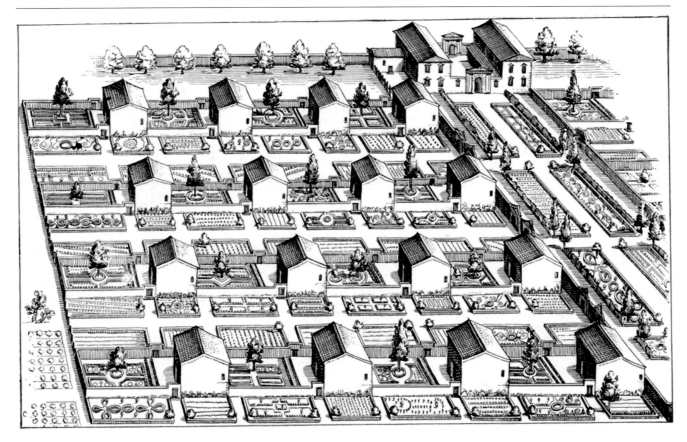

In this walled monastery near Turin, Italy, each monk had his own garden. The houses are reminiscent of a modern suburban neighborhood, without the cars. (Crisp 1924)

MONASTIC GARDENS

In the Middle Ages, a garden was simply an enclosed space. It was often a simple wattle fence that separated the outside world and formed the garden. In fact, the wattle fence itself, formed with flexible and abundant osier wood, became a symbol for a garden. The words *yard*, *garth*, *garden*, and the French *jardin* all come from the same Indo-European root word *gher*, meaning to grasp or enclose.

The concept of the outdoor garden room so popular in contemporary garden design is not a modern idea at all—it is as ancient as civilization itself. Many illuminated manuscripts and tapestries from the Middle Ages show the garden behind a wall or fence separate from the outside world. In these pleasure gardens, families played and strolled. These garden rooms were beautiful as well as practical, supplying a source of fresh food for the household within the protection of the high wall.

During the early Middle Age, monks created pockets of communities where they could devote themselves to quiet spiritual and intellectual

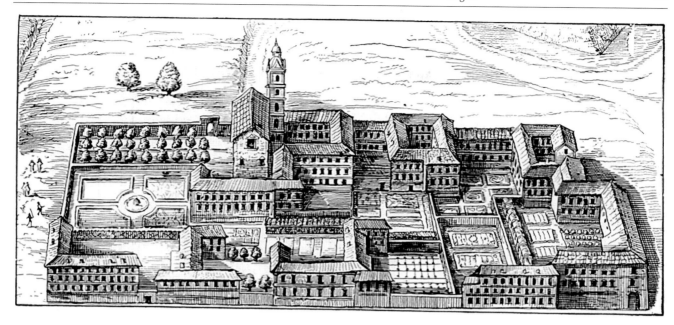

pursuits balanced with outdoor physical labor. The Benedictine monks had strict requirements to divide their time in equal allotments every day: meditation, study, and manual labor. Because the monasteries were secluded, protected, and separated from the outside world, the monks had to grow the food necessary for their sustenance. Seeds were highly valued as they were harvested, protected, and saved for the next growing season. Within the monastery walls a heritage of plants was preserved.

Within the enclosed space of the medieval monastery, the monks and their helpers tended vegetables and fruits laid out in geometric forms—squares, diamonds, and rectangles. The beds were usually clustered in symmetrical groups, sometimes forming larger patterns, as a mosaic is formed from tiles of varying colors and sizes. The raised beds were tended by hand, and no plot was wider than could be easily reached across by two people. The herbs, flowers, fruits, and vegetables in these early kitchen gardens were picked at perfect ripeness. Typically, the produce was near the kitchen: the cook's helper was within shouting distance as she or he collected the daily harvest. Cooking was extremely simple: vegetables, poultry, and meats were boiled. A roasted meat might appear on a feast day. Soup and bread were the basis of almost every single meal in the monastery.

In this monastic community in Turin, Italy, the cloister is evident as are the orchards and raised beds of the kitchen gardens. All the gardens lie within the enclosure of the buildings and walls. (Crisp 1924)

The ideal monastery in Saint Gall, Switzerland

Re-creating an authentic garden from the Middle Ages must be left partly to the imagination, but much can be learned from illuminated manuscripts,

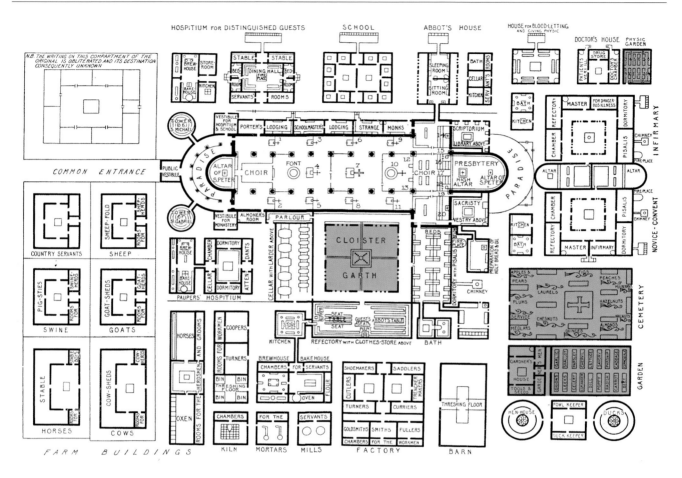

Plan of the Benedictine monastery of Saint Gall (green highlights the author's). (Crisp 1924)

remaining plant lists, letters, and other sources. One of the primary sources that illustrates the monastic garden is the plan of Saint Gall in Switzerland. This plan was not intended for a specific monastery, and it was never built; rather, it is an idealized plan drawn as a model circa 816 to 820 to illustrate the important elements in a ninth century monastery. From a landscape architecture view, the open spaces as they relate to the buildings and the plants in the gardens are of great interest. Would our kitchen gardens be complete if we planted what the self-sufficient monks grew? Within the walls are a cloister garden, a medicinal garden, a kitchen garden, and an orchard, which was also used as the burial garden.

Derived in form from the Roman peristyle, the cloister garth was a room open to the sky and enclosed by a colonnade. The cloister was always located on the south side of the church, where the garden could receive more sunlight. It symbolized God's light in the darkness to the monks; the color green also symbolized healing. A fountain of water typically appeared at the center of the cloister. The quadripartite form, as in the

Islamic gardens, represented the rivers flowing from the Garden of Eden. In the monastic gardens, the "four rivers" are intersecting pathways, with the water source serving as the central feature. The crossing paths also symbolized the wooden cross on which Jesus was crucified. Here the monks would meditate and pray. Christian symbolism in the late medieval period associated the *hortus conclusus* with the Virgin Mary; the concept also appears in the Song of Solomon 4:12: "A garden enclosed is my sister, my spouse; a spring shut up, a fountain sealed." This garden was also a reminder to the Christian of being called to be separate from the world.

In the plan of Saint Gall, the kitchen garden, with its raised beds, is conveniently placed next to the poultry barns for a continuous source of manure for improving the soil around the vegetables. The orchard, next to the hospital, is planted with a variety of fruit and nut trees: almond, fig, hazelnut, mulberry, peach, plum, quince, and walnut.

The medicinal garden was conveniently located near the doctor's house. The herbs and flowers were laid out in neat geometric rows of raised beds, each containing a single variety. Because of their knowledge of the healing arts, the monks were known as the physicians of the time and outsiders would come to the monastery to be healed. The monks would live out their lives within the monastery. When they became ill, the elderly monks were cared for within the walls; when they died, they were buried in the orchard, where the cycle of life and death was played out in the seasonal production of fruit—from the spring blossom to the dormant tree in the winter, a poignant message of death leading to life.

Charlemagne's *Capitulare de Villis*

Another primary source of medieval garden plants is the plant list included in Charlemagne's ninth century decree concerning towns. Charlemagne reigned as king and emperor of the Holy Roman Empire from 800 until his death in 814. He ruled over France, Belgium, Holland, and Switzerland; parts of Germany; Austria; more than half of Italy; and northern Spain. Toward the end of his reign, he decreed, in the *Capitulare de Villis*, that the crown lands in every city of the Empire should have a garden planted with all herbs as well as trees and fruits. The list (following pages) includes utilitarian culinary and medicinal flowers, herbs, vegetables, and fruits—but two plants at the top of the list were the lily and the rose, valued for their beauty and symbolism in the Christian church. These gardens were planted as a source of spiritual inspiration as well as nourishment for the body. The plant list gives insight into medieval gardens and provides a clue that the early kitchen gardens were planted for their beauty as well as for the produce.

PLANTS GROWN IN MONASTERIES

Althaea officinalis (marshmallow)

Borago officinalis (borage)

Calendula officinalis (pot marigold)

Fumaria officinalis (fumitory)

Hyssopus officinalis (hyssop)

Jasminum officinale (jasmine)

Lavandula officinalis (lavender)

Levisticum officinale (lovage)

Melissa officinalis (lemon balm)

Nasturtium officinale (watercress)

Paeonia officinalis (peony)

Pulmonaria officinalis (lungwort)

Rosa gallica var. *officinalis* (syn. *R. officinalis*) (rose)

Rosmarinus officinalis (rosemary)

Salvia officinalis (sage)

Saponaria officinalis (soapwort)

Symphytum officinale (comfrey)

Valeriana officinalis (valerian)

Verbena officinalis (vervain)

Capitulare de Villis
PLANT LIST

FLOWERS
flag iris
lily
rose

PHYSICAL HERBS
ammi (lace flower)
anise
asarabacca (hazelwort)
black cumin
bottle gourd
burdock
caper spurge
caraway
centaury
clary
colocynth
coriander
costmary
cumin
dill
dragons (tarragon)
fennel
fenugreek
houseleek
lovage
marshmallow
poppy
rosemary
rue
sage
savin (juniper)
southernwood
squills

SALADS
alexanders (angelica)
celery
chervil
chives
cress
cucumber
dittander (garden cress)
lettuce
melon
mustard
parsley
radish
rocket (arugula)

A drawing of Ab-Yberg in Switzerland shows 12 raised beds within the castle wall. (Crisp 1924)

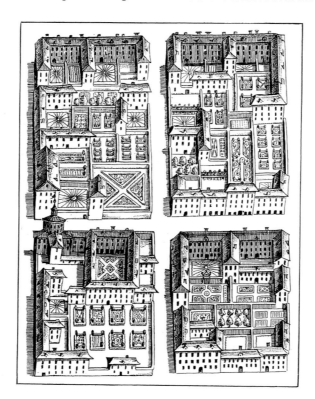

In the town of Turin, the buildings created the garden spaces. (Crisp 1924)

Garden as workshop

The Latin word *officinalis* means of or pertaining to a workshop, which in the Middle Ages also meant of or pertaining to a monastery. The English word *official*, an item kept in stock by a druggist, is a derivative. Plants we are growing in our own garden, such as *Salvia officinalis* or *Rosa gallica* var. *officinalis*, first grew in monastery gardens and were so named. When we grow any of the monastery plants, we can be reminded of the workshop concept: our gardens are grand experiments in climate, soil, pest control, and combinations of color, height, and texture. The workshop model suggests a process of change and intervention. The garden is never static: Always a corner of the planting bed can be improved by trying a new texture or color. Visual holes can be filled with temporary annuals. If we become weary of a color scheme, we change our minds and remove the disappointment. Our gardens, like the early monastery gardens, are an experimental laboratory. Mistakes will be made and deemed acceptable because we are one lesson closer to our ideal.

RENAISSANCE KITCHEN GARDENS

The transition from medieval gardens to Renaissance gardens was a matter of scale—the garden behind the wall became larger and more elaborate. Beginning with the Renaissance, French landscapes were reconfigured into large-scale geometries of pattern and shape. The newly rich middle class built smaller versions of castles and manor houses and laid out pleasure grounds around them. When the *châteaux* were needed less for defense, the garden also underwent a transition. The gardens were seen as an extension of the house and were divided into a series of green rooms connected with paved paths; the rooms consisted of the kitchen garden, the orchard, a bowling green, and an ordered maze. The garden and specifically the kitchen garden were meant to be seen from the *château*.

In contrast (with drastic culinary consequences), in England the kitchen garden was removed from the walls of the house and its courtyards. The 18th century landscape movement inspired by Lancelot "Capability" Brown promoted parklike settings for the estate, and all utilitarian plantings, such as the kitchen garden, were hidden from view. The English relegated the kitchen garden to a necessity, not a place to be enjoyed or even seen from the house. It was not the fashion of the day to see the "messy" working garden. William Woys Weaver, author and food historian, is convinced that the decline of English cookery can be traced to this influence and the separation of the cook from the daily connection to the *jardin potager*.

PULSES
broad bean
chickpea
kidney bean
pea

POTHERBS
beet
blite
catmint
chicory
colewort
endive
horse mint
kohlrabi
mallow
mint
orach (mountain spinach)
pennyroyal
savory
tansy
wild mint

ROOTS
carrot
garlic
leek
onion
parsnip
shallot
skirret

INDUSTRIAL PLANTS
madder
teasel

FRUIT TREES
apple
cherry
fig
medlar
mulberry
peach
pear
plum
quince
service

NUT TREES
almond
chestnut
hazelnut
pine
walnut

Garden with raised beds, 1542.
(Crisp 1924)

Monasteries and their gardens were abolished in 1539 in England and Wales, erasing many examples of inspiring historical connections of garden to kitchen.

Along with literature and clothing, the French nobility took food, and the kitchen garden, to new heights of complexity and extravagance, as seen in the gardens of Château de Villandry and Louis XIV's vegetable garden at Versailles, Le Potager du Roi. The French called these *jardin potagers* because these vegetables were ostensibly still destined for the soup pot but were sometimes planted simply for their color, texture, and shapes. French cooking became very refined and complicated but never lost sight of fresh local ingredients. The grand heritage of French cuisine is rooted in this connection of the kitchen to the garden.

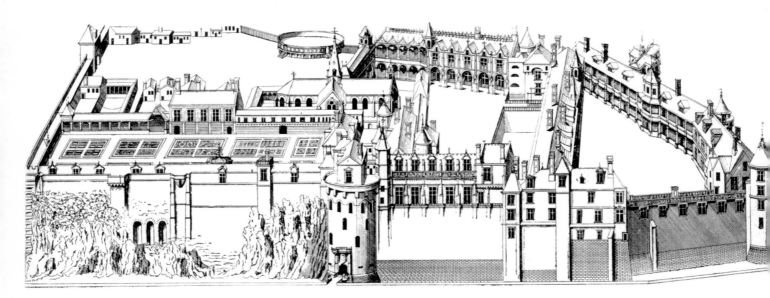

In Amboise, France, the geometric kitchen garden is within the *château* walls. (Crisp 1924)

CHAPTER TWO

Sources of Inspiration

IT IS ONLY NATURAL to begin our study of potager gardens in France, where vegetable gardening is an art form and the garden has always been intimately connected to the cuisine. A passion for great food begins with a love of growing that food—from preserving an heirloom seed, to cultivating the plants in the right place, to harvesting the succulent produce. Food is an adventure to be elegantly presented from seed to table. Gardeners and designers in France have been passionate about growing vegetables in a beautiful way for centuries, and three of the grandest Renaissance potager gardens in the world are here; one of these gardens

At Bois Richeux, a medieval garden south of Paris, a wicker plate protects a squash from touching the wet soil.

A comparison of size of potager gardens: from left to right, Le Potager du Roi, the potager at Saint-Jean de Beauregard, the potager at Villandry, and a typical American suburban residential lot. (Note that only the ornamental kitchen garden at Villandry is shown for comparison, not the ornamental flower and water gardens.)

was directly inspired by the monastic, medieval garden, and the others were indirectly inspired. Although vast in scale, they have served as inspiration for generations of potager gardeners cultivating herbs and vegetables on their own properties.

Our study begins with two modern potager gardens designed with elements from medieval gardens. One garden location is an old monastery and the other is an old farm. Each of the buildings in these gardens dates to the medieval time period and the design and plant use acknowledge this connection. These gardens are inspiring in their modern re-creation of old themes—a blending of old and new, ancient and modern. The scale and size of these gardens is something we can relate to in creating our suburban potagers as designed spaces that provide our tables with fresh, seasonal produce. Each of these gardens offers us wisdom in applying great design principles to our own residential and restaurant gardens.

PRIEURÉ D'ORSAN
A modern monastic garden

The entrance into this monastery is unobtrusive—a simple doorway in an ancient stone wall. Yet, as you step through the threshold, you are immediately surrounded with the green serenity of the garden and the feeling that the rest of the world grew around this place, while here the purity of a life connected to the earth was preserved. This garden is the vision of two architects, Sonia Lesot and Patrice Taravella, and a gardener, Gilles Guillot, who transformed an ancient, deteriorated monastery into a modern garden that evokes the simplicity and dependence on the land of ages past.

The central green parterre of the garden at Prieuré d'Orsan is flanked by the enclosed hallways that surround the area. Wheat, beans, and cabbage are rotated through the years.

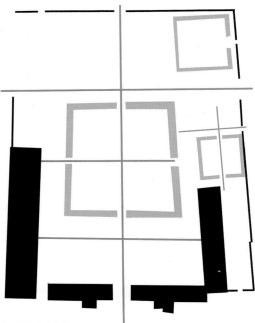

Plan view of the Prieuré d'Orsan garden, showing the axial layout of the central garden and the edges of walls and buildings.

The Prieuré d'Orsan garden of simples features medicinal herbs grown in medieval times.

This is not a restoration or an exact replica of a medieval garden but an interpretation of a medieval garden based on extensive research into early monastic gardens. The principles that drove the design solution were clearly articulated before the artists drew up the plan. This "big idea" enabled the designers to accomplish the creation of an earthly paradise that evokes the mood of a healing monastery garden. The vision plan, according to Taravella, was to create a self-sufficient way of life based on agriculture, as in the Middle Ages; to use enclosure to create a microcosm where plants,

With a backdrop of evergreens, this osier wood bench provides a secluded place to rest while walking the paths at Prieuré d'Orsan.

animals, and people live in harmony; and to create a garden that provides spiritual food and peace of mind in addition to food for the body.

The theme for the restoration interpretation is appropriate because of the history surrounding the site. The architects discovered the crumbling walls of a priory built in 1107 by the founder of the religious order of Fontevraud. Through the centuries, the buildings continued to be used as a priory until after the French Revolution at the end of the 18th century, when the property was used as a farm and quarry before being abandoned and overgrown with brambles. The architects used the existing buildings to create the space of the new garden. These old stone buildings form the walls of the garden; they are the beginning point of the framework that creates the garden.

All of the garden spaces are inside the buildings' U-shaped enclosure. A mature oak forest provides the final edge to the space. The central foundation to the plan is the cloister garden, with a fountain at its center, which lies on the main axis of the gardens, linking the porch and the original access to the priory to the oldest tree remaining from the ancient garden. A stone wall also surrounds the entire garden, connecting to the buildings and completing the rectangular enclosure that creates an internal paradise.

Hornbeam hedges, with trimmed, round openings, are used to create additional walls that separate the garden into rooms and hallways. The "windows" in the hedges allow the visitor to catch a glimpse of the next garden room, creating a sense of mysterious anticipation for those who glimpse some but not all of the next room and the growing delights it contains. Hallways paved with cobbles connect the rooms. Although the entire garden is a potager—filled with edible plants, roses, flowers, berries, and fruit trees—a separate designated kitchen garden is created in the form of a circular maze with a path made of wooden planks. The maze is reminiscent of the labyrinths the monks would walk in meditation and prayer. The seasonal walls of this maze are created with annual flowers, such as airy white cosmos and a mix of tall-growing vegetables.

The hornbeam hedges form multiple rooms at Prieuré d'Orsan. The smaller enclosed garden room is a "secret" garden, with special plants for exclusive use by overnight guests.

Cobblestones form the floor in this enclosed hallway at Prieuré d'Orsan.

The fountain is in the center of the cloister garden at Prieuré d'Orsan; covered bowers are placed at the four corners of the formal space.

Getting lost in the maze kitchen garden at Prieuré d'Orsan wouldn't be so bad, with sweet cherry tomatoes for sustenance.

Taravella is not only an architect of the master plan of the garden, the restoration of the buildings, and the interiors, but he is also an accomplished chef, happy to prepare a meal for those who stay the night. All of the meals are created from the wealth of produce in the orchard and kitchen garden. In season, fresh currants, raspberries, black raspberries,

Rhubarb is blanched in willow baskets, with nasturtiums allowed to climb freely at Prieuré d'Orsan.

Multiple layers of enclosure form this part of the garden room at Prieuré d'Orsan: the trees in the background, the hornbeam hedge, and the sculptural trellis. The colors are simple and soothing—green and white with punctuations of orange.

strawberries, bilberries, and gooseberries will be offered; out of season, homemade jams and chutneys from the same will accompany the plate. The produce is grown right outside the kitchen door, intermingled in the design of the overall garden. Visitors who stay the night can choose a room that overlooks the main garden or one that has a private, enclosed "secret" garden planted with an individual color theme.

At Bois Richeux, spiral evergreens announce the front door of the old farmhouse in formal boxwood squares. An informal patchwork of lavender creates a pleasant balance to the hard edge.

BOIS RICHEUX
A medieval farm

Bois Richeux is one of the oldest farms in France. In 1178, it was one of the first farms to be owned and worked by a farmer and his family. Throughout the Middle Ages, it was an important fortified farm with a manor, chapel, tithe barn, and dovecote. The farmhouse, barn, and storage buildings form the space of the garden and clearly define the garden's edges. Hornbeam hedges and trees complete the wall of the space. The garden has an axis, but it is not completely symmetrical in its layout.

Sixty-eight raised beds filled with aromatic culinary and medicinal plants are laid out in a grid pattern. This repetition gives a modern feel to the garden, like a Piet Mondrian painting, with colored squares and boxes laid on the ground. The beds are edged with a variety of materials, including clipped boxwood, stone, wood, and wattle fencing. This hardscape gives structure to the garden, while the vegetables, herbs, and flowers are laid

The Bois Richeux potager space is created with the old farmhouse as an edge. The grid pattern of the beds is the framework of the strong design, and the plants in the beds are grouped informally.

Wood structures and glass cloches are decorative as well as useful additions to the beds at Bois Richeux.

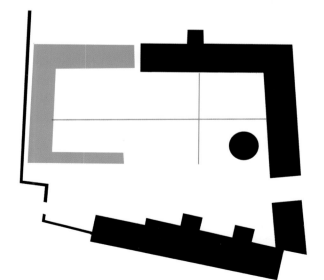

Plan view of the layout of the Bois Richeux garden and buildings.

An axial view from the grape arbor to the opening in the hedge at Bois Richeux.

At Bois Richeux, lavender and other herbs are allowed to sprawl over the formal edges of the bed, creating a pleasant design contrast between formality and unconstraint.

out in an informal arrangement in the beds and sprawl over the neat edges. The square beds are about 4 by 4 ft. (1 by 1 m), and each herb or flower can easily be reached for snipping and maintenance. Rustic wood structures placed in the center of the beds hold climbing vines.

The small scale of this garden and the house make its design applicable to residential or urban gardens. No front lawn here—the beds of herbs and vegetables are placed in rows near the house without an unnatural transition space. The expansive, rhythmic checkerboard of colors is an effective and modern design element. The garden contains a hornbeam cloister, a secret garden of love, and a room for meditation, all symbols from the Middle Ages.

An old wooden tub is placed at the center of two crossing axes in the Bois Richeux garden.

Wood structures support the trunks of the trees, and a small opening in the hedge gives a view of the open fields beyond the Bois Richeux potager.

Herbs are allowed to grow freely between the cobblestones.

CHÂTEAU DE VILLANDRY
A *château* garden

The potager at the Château de Villandry is the most famous vegetable garden in the world. Here the lowly vegetable is elevated to an art form. Each type of vegetable is selected for its color and texture as it contributes to the overall design. Blue-green vertical leeks, purple ruffled basil, bright green lettuce, and dark green curly parsley are painted onto the landscape. Each variety fulfills an aesthetic and culinary purpose. The kitchen garden at Villandry contains overlays of medieval, French, and Italian Renaissance gardens with the formality and monumentality of a French garden. The layout is based on medieval monastery designs from hundreds of years ago, yet the formal lines, simple rows, and blocks of color appeal to contemporary tastes. The scale of the potager is monumental, but it offers lessons that can be applied to the small-scale residential garden.

The *château* was completed in 1536 and was the last of the large *châteaux* built on the banks of the Loire during the Renaissance. In the 19th century, the original traditional gardens were destroyed to create an English-style park around the *château*. Joachim Carvallo, great-grandfather of the present owners, bought the *château* in 1906 and began to restore the gardens from 16th century plans, devoting his life to this endeavor. This restoration coincided with his conversion to Catholicism and his interest in monastic gardens and symbols. The cross pattern is evident in the layout of the beds, which feature the

The rooms in the Château de Villandry overlook the colorful potager.

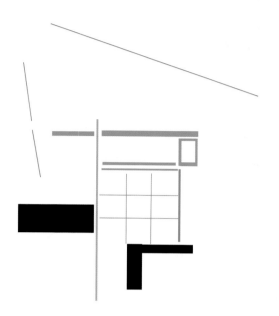

Ground plan of the layout of the gardens and buildings at Villandry.

Even a potager as large as Villandry has layers of enclosure, such as walls and hedges.

Roses pruned as standards are reminiscent of the monks who once labored in the monastery gardens at Château de Villandry

geometric forms typical in monastic gardens. Monks, of course, planted roses in their gardens, and the roses in the vegetable beds recall this tradition; the symmetrical design of the roses growing on 6 ft. (2 m) high standards represents the monks themselves working in the vegetable garden.

The three acre ornamental kitchen garden is on the lowest of three terraces, where it is most protected from the elements. It consists of nine equal squares separated by wide alleys. Each of the nine squares contains a different geometrical pattern formed with vegetables of different colors and textures. At the intersection of paths is a bower covered with roses and jasmine. A fountain is placed in the center of the intersection, and another fountain appears in the center of each of the nine squares—used by the early gardener to fill his watering bucket before irrigation was available. Now the stone fountains contains urns, which serve as focal points in each square. The geometric beds are separated by crushed gravel walkways that are 30 in. (76 cm) wide.

One of the nine patterned squares in the Château de Villandry potager, each bordered by low espaliered fruit hedges.

The kitchen garden was also influenced by gardens of Italy, as reflected in the fountains, bowers, and flower beds. The dwarf boxwood edging adds structure to the wintertime garden. Two plantings occur at Villandry: one in spring and one in summer. Forty species of vegetables are used annually. The design of the vegetables changes with each planting, and plants are arranged according to color and the horticultural requirements of a three-year crop rotation.

Each of three separate themed gardens resides on a different plateau. The highest and most remote level from the *château* is the irrigation pond and water garden. The second and central plateau contains the ornamental flower garden with boxwood borders. On the lowest and most protected level is the ornamental kitchen garden. Each garden is enclosed by covered *allées*, either pruned lindens or trellised grapevines, so each garden feels separate from the others with a definite boundary. The three gardens are themselves enclosed. To the west, the wall is formed by the town and old church. To the east is the belvedere, with the woods in the background forming the boundary or wall. The northern wall is created by the stables and tool shed, which also serve to protect the potager from wind and cold. The southern wall, at the highest point, is the surrounding woods and countryside.

The medicinal garden is separate from the vegetable garden, as it was in medieval monastery gardens, and contains herbs and flowers surrounded by a low boxwood border and taller clipped boxwood. These beds are circular

At Château de Villandry, calamint, lavender, and rhubarb grow in the medicinal herb garden, which was traditionally separated from the kitchen garden.

The old church and town form a western edge to the potager at Château de Villandry.

with a quadripartite center path. The herbs and flowers are allowed to sprawl naturally and are much less formal than the vegetables in the kitchen garden, which are planted in neat rows.

The ornamental kitchen garden at Villandry is inspiring, even for the small residential gardener. First of all, the vegetables are beautiful, with varying colors and textures that serve the purpose of pleasing the eye, even if they are never eaten. Purple basil is as ornamental in the garden as any annual flower. The geometric designs can be used as a template in any small garden to plant edges of boxwood with tight rows of vegetables planted inside. The result looks uncluttered, sleek, and minimalist.

Though the ornamental kitchen garden at Villandry is massive in scale, the concept of the *hortus conclusus* is prevalent; we still find the enclosed garden. The garden is meant to be enjoyed in many ways—something to keep in mind when designing our potagers. It is enjoyed internally, like any other ornamental garden, surrounding the visitor with the ambiance created from the walls and the plants. It is also enjoyed on a practical level, for the harvest and taste of the vegetables. Finally, the garden is enjoyed externally, as one would view a beautiful painting—by standing apart from the picture and looking at it. The varying shapes and patterns of color are designed to be enjoyed from the upper floors of the house or *château*.

No transition separates the house and the kitchen garden at Château de Villandry.

The walkway forms a transition between the Château de Villandry ornamental garden and the kitchen garden.

The Château de Villandry potager is on the lowest of three levels, where the vegetables are most protected.

A purple border of annuals forms the edge of the rows of vegetables at Saint-Jean de Beauregard.

SAINT-JEAN DE BEAUREGARD
A Renaissance *château* garden

The private estate of Saint-Jean de Beauregard is open for public visits to the grounds; here, only about 40 miles from Paris, is a glimpse into self-sufficient 17th century French estate life. The building of the large sandstone *château* was begun in 1612. The current owner, Muriel de Curel, began restoring the potager in 1984, and in eight years she transformed the garden into an historic French monument. The five acre garden is surrounded by a spectacular 12 ft. (4 m) stone wall that effectively creates a secluded world of fruits, flowers, and fragrance.

The estate includes a large walled potager for fresh fruits and vegetables; a large, round wooden dovecote that supplied the early owners with meat and eggs; and a park surrounding the gardens and house. The potager, with its surrounding stone wall, is a fine example of a Renaissance kitchen garden, laid out in a decorative manner—grand and elegant with espaliered trees and swaths of lawn between the beds. The wall, originally built for security to keep out roving animals and bandits, also creates a microclimate for the growing plants, effectively screening wind the distance of ten times its height to protect borderline hardy perennials. The flowers and plants along each face of the wall are either sun-loving or shade-loving, depending on where they are planted. Sun-loving perennials, vines, apricot trees, fig trees, and kiwi grow along the south face. Hellebores, honeysuckle, and hostas are planted on the north face. Roses, shrubs, and perennials are on

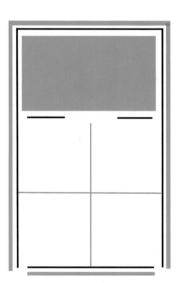

Plan view of Saint-Jean de Beauregard.

Fruit trees line the open lawn in the orchard at Saint-Jean de Beauregard.

the eastern side of the wall, and currant bushes and clematis grow along the western facing wall.

The quadripartite layout and use of color in the garden is typical of 17th century kitchen gardens. Two primary paths divide the garden into four main squares. These wide, crushed gravel strolling paths are lined with espaliered apple and pear trees, irises, and peonies. The crossing paths meet at a central pond, which originally served as the primary watering source for the garden. The four squares are also divided by crossing grass pathways. This creates 16 vegetable plots, each containing an edge of mixed flowers. Each group of four squares contains a different color palette, creating four crosses of flowers: blue, yellow, white, and pink. The vegetables are planted in neat rows intermingled with herbs within the colorful flower borders.

Muriel de Curel is committed to sustainable farming practices in her potager. Each year, four of the small squares are planted with clover. This cover crop is a green fertilizer and prevents depletion

At Saint-Jean de Beauregard, an espaliered apple tree grows along the sunny face of the wall.

of nutrients from the soil. The clover is allowed to grow and then tilled into the soil to restore nutrients and allow the soil a rest from producing vegetables. The squares planted with clover are rotated annually, and the vegetable families are also rotated. Rare and unusual varieties of vegetables are planted every year—12 varieties of pumpkins, *pois carré* (square peas), and black potatoes, as well as many varieties of antique roses and annual flowers.

Planted along the axis of the crushed gravel path is an interesting spacing of plants. Peonies, cleome, and gaura are planted alternately and repeatedly, forming a rhythmic *allée* of color. During September, the blooming pink cleome and white gaura create a pleasant cadence of step-step pink, step-step white, all along the path. In the spring, with the peonies in bloom, the color and experience would be just as rhythmically striking but unique to its season. These plants bloom at different times of the year, ensuring a variety of color and experience throughout the growing season.

The old cistern at the center of the quadripartite garden was the original watering source for Saint-Jean de Beauregard.

Red amaranth and green Italian parsley grow in neat rows at Saint-Jean de Beauregard, while yellow mums add a contrasting color. Ancient espaliered fruit trees line the rows.

The mix of yellow and orange flowers borders the vegetables at Saint-Jean de Beauregard.

Allium grows among other flowers that surround the vegetables at Saint-Jean de Beauregard.

Perfect grapes are kept at the ideal temperature in the greenhouse at Saint-Jean de Beauregard.

The walkway at Saint-Jean de Beauregard looks good all year long with a succession of blooming plants, including peonies, cleome, and gaura.

Le Potager du Roi is enclosed by the city, whose buildings, beyond the wall, form a visual boundary.

LE POTAGER DU ROI AT CHÂTEAU VERSAILLES
A *château* potager garden

Le potager du roi literally means the kitchen garden of the king. Not an average garden of the 17th century, Le Potager du Roi was the extravagant kitchen garden of Louis XIV, the Sun King. His palace at Versailles and the surrounding landscape, designed by André Le Notre, were very much a political statement, meant to show the public and all of Europe his power and dominion over nature. He required no less in his vegetable garden. This spectacular functional kitchen garden was to supply the court with specialty varieties of fruits and vegetables using the most advanced technology of the day.

Le Potager du Roi was designed by the architect Jules Hardouin-Mansart and built in the years 1678 to 1683. Jean-Baptiste de la Quintinie, a lawyer and a lover of ancient readings on the art of growing plants, was commissioned by the king to turn swampland into a fruitful garden. He organized the underground drainage and concentrated his efforts on building up the quality of the soil with manure from the stables. As a result

At the entrance gate into Le Potager du Roi, the high wall is the first layer of protection for the vegetables.

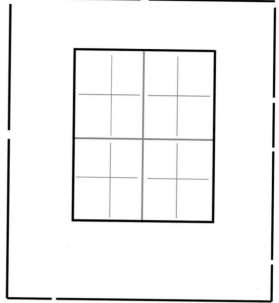

Plan view of Le Potager du Roi.

of the well-drained fertile soil and the protection provided by the walls, the potager produced asparagus in December, strawberries in March, cucumbers and peas in April, and figs from June to October—whatever the king desired. History tells us the king loved his *petit pois*.

The scale of the garden is vast, now encompassing 22 acres in the center of an urban area, just down the street from the Palace of Versailles. The garden is layered with a series of walls: Visually, the surrounding buildings in the distance create a wall, and the mature trees in the adjacent park also create an edge. A large stone wall with gates surrounds the potager. When the visitor enters the garden at street level, the view is of the central part of the garden, which is about 12 ft. (4 m) lower than street level. All of this was ingeniously designed to protect the fragile seedlings and create the ideal environment for growing fruits and vegetables.

The layout of the garden is similar to the earlier Renaissance potager at Saint-Jean de Beauregard; it shares the central basin and two main crossing paths, which divide the garden into quarters, each of which is also divided into quarters, for a total of 16 main garden squares. However, the king's vegetable garden is four times larger than the Saint-Jean de Beauregard potager. Everything in Le Potager du Roi is neat, rectilinear, axial, symmetrical, and grand. Even the crushed gravel pathways are wide enough for a truck to drive into the center of the garden.

Other gardens surround these 16 squares. At one time, 29 additional gardens were protected behind high walls and connected by tunnels, but today fewer gardens exist. These garden rooms serve a variety of purposes: some are especially for growing fruits, and the flat, ancient espaliered trees

Inside the walled garden of Le Potager du Roi are a series of sunken walled gardens that offer another layer of protection from the elements for the fruits, herbs, and vegetables.

are planted close together in rows forming tall, narrow planes of green; some of the rooms are for growing herbs; others are for growing tropical fruits.

The gardens are currently managed by students of the École Nationale Supérieure du Paysage, the French school of landscape architecture. Among other things, the students help continue the art of pruning the 5000 espaliered fruit trees in this living history laboratory. Fifty tons of fruit from 300 different varieties are harvested yearly. Fifty varieties of ancient and traditional vegetables produce 20 tons of vegetables annually. It is possible to purchase some of this rare produce in the nearby shop.

Le Potager du Roi was created to be a grand vegetable garden—beautiful as well as productive, using the most advanced knowledge of fruit and vegetable production in the 17th century. Despite the advancements of our modern age, we can be influenced by these ancient gardens in the way we grow food and the way we think about food. Our potager gardens should be as diverse as possible—the more varieties we grow the better. Rare varieties should be included to preserve the heritage of seed before it is lost. Ornamental and practical vegetable gardens belong in the middle of our cities to provide some green respite from the gray urbanity.

Le Potager du Roi is a blend of old and new; ancient fruit trees in their perfect form contrast with the newly planted lettuce seedlings.

CHAPTER THREE

Design Lessons from Three American Gardens

THE AMERICAN GARDENS presented in this chapter are unique specialty kitchen gardens. Each is adapted to the needs of the owner, the landscape, and the climate zone, and each is beautifully designed. These private potager gardens in Texas, Maryland, and Vermont are extensions of the owners' homes and kitchens and are good examples of the variety of growing conditions available in the United States. Each also represents a design aesthetic that transcends climate zones and demonstrates practical use and design for every edible garden. These gardens teach us lessons on layout, enclosure, design, and combinations and varieties of plants. All are critical elements to consider before you actually build a kitchen garden to ensure the result is a space where you and your guests will linger. Consider the plantings and designs in the Antique Rose Emporium, Barclay garden, and the garden at North Hill as guides that you can use in dreaming about and creating your own garden.

ANTIQUE ROSE EMPORIUM
Parsley, sage, rosemary, and roses

Mike Shoup, owner of the Antique Rose Emporium in Brenham, Texas, is passionate about roses—not the fussy, finicky prize roses bred for a single, grafted bloom, but the hardy, antique historical roses that thrive whether they are tended or ignored. These roses grow on their own root stocks and have retained their wonderful fragrance.

Old roses make a great addition to the potager for many reasons. Antique variety roses connect us to the early monastery gardens, where they were

56

grown for their beauty and medicinal qualities. Roses also contribute to the architecture and structure of the kitchen garden and can be used in a variety of ways. They produce colorful petals for delicate flavoring in soups, salads, and ice cream and large edible hips for salads or snacking. These carefree roses integrate well with other flowers, herbs, and vegetables in the garden and complement the concept of the potager as an attractive mixed garden that produces seasonal food as well as flowers for the table.

The tenacity and beauty of these survivors in the intense heat and dry conditions of climate Zone 8 so intrigued Mike that he began (with permission) collecting cuttings from old roses found along highways and cemeteries. He was one of the original "Texas rose rustlers" who were motivated to preserve the heritage of these resilient plants so that their genes would not be lost. Their names often forgotten, these tough plants left behind by a past gardener thrive and bloom, even if no one has cared for them.

The Antique Rose Emporium displays roses in inspiring demonstration gardens. These garden vignettes help us understand how we can include

The pink shrub rose 'Duchesse de Brabant' mingles with blue salvia at the Antique Rose Emporium.

At the Antique Rose Emporium, edible borders of curly parsley line the mixed bed along the fence with the pale pink shrub rose 'Souvenir de la Malmaison'.

roses in our gardens, right along with the peppers and tomatoes, for a truly mixed garden. The demonstration gardens were not created as potager gardens, exactly, but we can borrow ideas from the way these roses are used in creating our potagers. Gardeners who live in a climate zone similar to this Zone 8 locale will find that many varieties of roses thrive in a harsh climate when other plants won't. This makes old roses a good choice for long-lasting color.

Roses connect to the past

The rose originally found in medieval monastery gardens was *Rosa gallica* var. *officinalis*, grown for its symbolism, medicinal qualities, and fragrance. This variety prefers a more temperate climate, but other varieties of European roses thrive in the heat of Texas. Mike says that about 90 percent of the roses he grows come from stock originally developed in France.

Roses remind us that the utilitarian garden should also be enjoyed for its beauty and that kitchen gardens can be places of meditation and solace as well as sources of food. Growing roses in the potager among vegetables and herbs is a way to connect historically with medieval monastery gardens, but old roses also connect us with our own past. Many of these rose varieties were grown by our grandparents and their parents. Sometimes the fragrance of an old rose can trigger fond memories of loved ones or places we have traveled. Fragrance is part of the memory we create in the garden, and not many flowers can compare with the fragrance of an old rose.

Roses as architectural elements

Antique roses are not only carefree, beautiful, and fragrant, but they serve a variety of functional and structural purposes in the potager. Roses become architecture in three primary ways: when used as a feature, when used as a wall, and when used as a gateway. Depending on the height and habit of the variety, roses can be a special feature planted in a mixed bed in the potager, a living wall surrounding the potager to provide enclosure, or a gateway announcing the entrance into the potager.

Sometimes roses play the star role as the feature in the mixed garden, providing eye-catching color for a brief moment of display before fading back, so other perennials and herbs can be the focus. A single rose bush at

The large cabbage blooms of 'Enfant de France' (Zones 5 to 9) attract attention in any garden. This shrub rose serves the role of a feature in the garden at the Antique Rose Emporium.

the terminus of a path or at the edge of a raised bed acts as a focal point, drawing the eye to a burst of color.

When planted in the mixed vegetable bed, the best rose variety will be in scale with the size of the potager. A small, enclosed garden requires a rose that will not overgrow its designated area. Larger varieties can be planted as features outside the enclosed garden, but they can still contribute to the visual beauty of the potager. Their large size will attract attention, and their subtle or bright colors can be seen through a lattice or picket fence.

Sometimes roses form a garden wall and provide the edge of separation between the kitchen garden and other garden rooms. A fine example of this is the shrub rose from China, *Rosa chinensis* 'Old Blush'. This is the original shrub rose that was bred with the European roses to develop everblooming roses in a variety of colors. Shrub roses alone can grow high enough to create the enclosed garden, or they can be planted along a fence to create a low wall. Plant shrub roses a few feet apart to create a hedge; this living wall will produce fragrant, colorful blooms throughout the growing season with a backdrop of green, disease-resistant foliage. In the fall, many varieties will produce a new burst of color with orange to red hips that supply more vitamin C than an orange. Hips that are not made into tea or eaten can be brought into the house for arrangements. The edible wall is another important layer in the formation of the designed potager.

Rose Recommendations

Rose expert Mike Shoup suggests the following hybrids, which make great hedge roses on a wall: 'Monsieur Tiller' is hardy in Zones 7 to 9 with fragrant, rose to salmon-colored blooms. A fragrant pink hybrid, 'Old Blush', is hardy in Zones 6 to 9 and forms edible hips. 'Perle d'Or' is a yellow, fragrant hybrid that is hardy in Zones 6 to 9.

These roses can be used as an informal hedge or wall: 'Pinkie' (Cl) is a pink, fragrant hybrid that is hardy in Zones 6 to 9. 'Danae', hardy in Zones 6 to 9, is pale yellow, fragrant, and forms hips. 'Penelope' is hardy in Zones 6 to 9; the pale pink hybrid is fragrant and forms hips.

The following vigorous everblooming climbers are suitable for a gateway to the potager: 'New Dawn' is hardy from Zones 5 to 9; its pale pink blooms are fragrant. Light pink and fragrant 'Cécile Brünner' (Cl) is hardy in Zones 6 to 9. The fragrant white hybrid 'Lamarque' is hardy in Zones 7 to 9.

These roses work as potager features, mixing well with herbs, flowers, and vegetables: 'Gruss an Aachen' is a pale pink, scented hybrid that is hardy in Zones 5 to 9. 'Rouletti' is a lilac-pink hybrid hardy in Zones 6 to 9. 'Marie Pavie' is hardy in Zones 5 to 9 and features fragrant white blooms.

Rosa chinensis 'Old Blush' can be used to create a living hedge about 5 ft. (1.5 m) tall, producing large, orange edible hips.

Rosa chinensis 'Old Blush', hardy in Zones 6 to 9, is an everblooming, carefree, fragrant shrub rose.

Climbing roses can play the structural role in the potager, but they require support from an existing fence, trellis, or wall. Planting climbing varieties near a fence surrounding the potager and allowing them to sprawl along the fence adds fragrance and color to the garden. Climbers can cover sheds and garages that may be at the edge of the potager, helping to enhance the volume of the space; the blooming roses add a beautiful face to the existing building.

When the climbers cover an arbor or climb posts, the color, height, and fragrance of the roses create an entrance or gateway through which we enter into the potager paradise. Featuring roses at the entrance to the kitchen garden highlights the importance of the entry as the beginning of the potager experience.

'Crepuscule' is a climbing noisette rose. Trained to climb on a fence, this apricot-colored rose forms a living wall to enclose the vegetable garden.

Rosa 'American Beauty' (Cl) will cover arbors to create a fragrant entrance gateway into the garden. Imagine this rose on two pillars framing the entrance to the potager.

Rosa 'Zéphirine Drouhin' (Zones 6 to 9) is an heirloom climbing rose for trellises and arbors. This repeat bloomer can be used as a gateway into the potager and can climb on fences to provide a backdrop of color.

Roses integrate with flowers and vegetables

Mike describes his garden not as a rose garden, but a garden with roses in it. The roses are not the only attraction in the garden, but they are an important part of the garden's ecosystem. These roses are not sprayed with pesticides or antifungal agents to kill pests and diseases, so the health of the plants depends on a variety of natural strategies. While a single monoculture of roses in the garden would be vulnerable to a single pest or fungus, a wide variety of plants grown together invites predatory insects, birds, and butterflies that feed on harmful insects. Since the roses are not treated with chemicals, the rose petals and hips as well as the herbs and vegetables can be used as edible garnishes. The diverse demonstration gardens at the Antique Rose Emporium grow a combination of edible plants—Swiss chard,

The fragrant pink shrub rose 'Carnation' grows well in the mixed border of squash and blue delphinium along a fence at the Antique Rose Emporium. Hardy in Zones 7 to 9, it blooms continuously.

Chives, parsley, calendula, and lavender grow in this mixed herb garden at the Antique Rose Emporium. Inverted clay pots create a simple, decorative divider.

ornamental peppers, hot peppers, curly parsley, Italian flat leaf parsley, bronze fennel, rosemary, lavender, sage, salvia, poppies, kale, larkspur, daisies, dill, squash, grasses, boxwood, juniper, cypress, and, of course, roses.

The red foliage of annual 'Bright Lights' Swiss chard mixes well with lavender in the Antique Rose Emporium garden.

Spring, summer, fall, winter

March, April, and May are glorious months in south-central Texas. The roses at the Antique Rose Emporium reach their peak of color in early April (as do the bluebonnets along the way). The roses are in full bloom and mingle well with the annual herbs, flowers, and vegetables that have enjoyed about eight weeks of growth since the last killing frost. The first harvest of the tomatoes and peppers is in May.

June, July, and August is a time of languishing rest for the garden. Plants go dormant for a time, as it is just too hot to grow. The rose bushes remain green, but they stop flowering. Mike says that nighttime becomes important in the garden, as it might get cool enough for a stroll to enjoy any white, fragrant plants that are in bloom, reflecting the moonlight.

In September, October, and November, the garden rejuvenates and many of the roses bloom again. A second harvest of vegetables occurs— heat-loving peppers and okra do especially well this time of year. The

Ornamental peppers, such as these upright chilies, range from mild to hot and are beautiful as well as edible. They glow when planted next to rosemary, which is hardy in Texas.

temperatures have cooled, and lettuce, cabbages, and pumpkins can be harvested along with bouquets of roses for the Thanksgiving holiday table.

In mild winter months, many cool-season crops will endure. At this time, the structure of the garden is evident, and fences, trellises, and evergreens become important visual elements in the garden. The Antique Rose Emporium may not have snow for Christmas, but fragrant roses often grace the garden and the table even at this time of year.

BARCLAY GARDEN
A modern *hortus conclusus*

As with many American cities, the Washington Metroplex suburban landscape of Potomac, Maryland (Zone 6), is expanding into the surrounding farmland. Sprouting houses are the new crop that encircles the 19th century farm that has been Gay and Tony Barclay's home since the early 1980s. When the couple searched for property, Gay hoped to create her own oasis in the midst of the encroaching suburban development. She wanted a special place that would preserve the heritage of the old blacksmith's cottage and the memory of the nearby C&O Canal. She wanted a place where she could entertain friends, pick lettuce from the garden, and serve dinner while they relaxed with a glass of wine. She also wanted an outdoor kitchen in the midst of a garden haven, where she could combine her love of cooking with her love of growing beautiful plants.

Gay visited many potagers in France and Rosemary Verey's Barnsley House garden in England; she also studied landscape design and attended L'Academie cooking school in Paris, but she says her love of fresh, authentic food comes "honestly." She grew up on a farm in Indiana, where her family grew fresh produce, and she was lucky enough to eat corn, beans, and lettuce straight from the garden. When she headed for college, her mother sent with her a suitcase filled with freshly cut asparagus—heaven forbid she should eat anything canned or frozen.

Gay knew she didn't want a sprawling vegetable garden—the kind that needs constant maintenance and looks rather messy. She wanted a neat and tidy garden with raised beds, a garden that would be integrated into the design of her entire property.

The garden wall and living spaces

The couple's land gently slopes down at the edge of the property, and this is where Gay started building a wall. She hired a stone mason to build a 4 ft. (1 m) stone retaining wall and create steps down into this sunken and

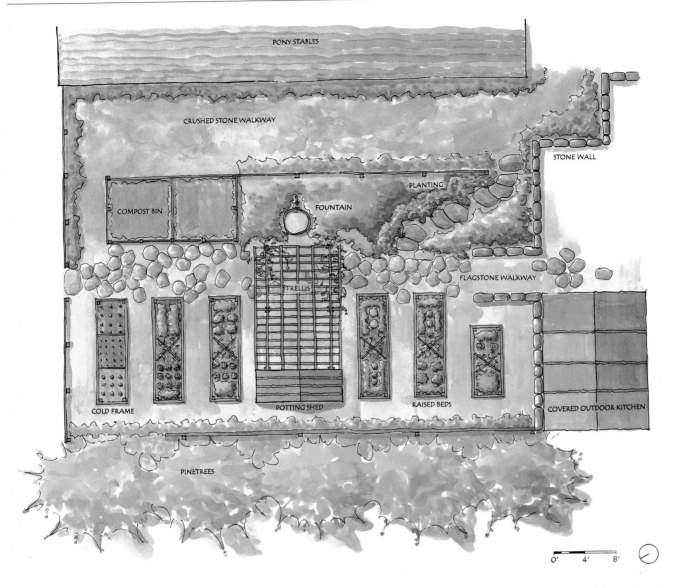

PONY STABLES

CRUSHED STONE WALKWAY

STONE WALL

COMPOST BIN

PLANTING

FOUNTAIN

TRELLIS

FLAGSTONE WALKWAY

COLD FRAME

POTTING SHED

RAISED BEDS

COVERED OUTDOOR KITCHEN

PINE TREES

0'   4'   8'

The plan view of the Barclay potager, designed by the landscape architecture firm Clinton and Associates. (Rendered by Jennifer R. Bartley)

enclosed space. With the primary element in place, Gay called her friend and former design teacher, landscape architect Sandy Clinton, to clarify and focus the design of the garden.

Sandy visited the space on a sweltering summer day and immediately articulated the need in the garden for shade, water, and plants. This began a collaboration between client and landscape architect that has resulted in an enchanting, delightful, award-winning oasis. Clinton and Associates in Hyattsville, Maryland, designed the layout, structures, and hardscape elements in the Barclay garden. The result is a collection of outdoor garden rooms that invite visitors to explore, for although each space is clearly articulated, the curving stone pathways and the variety of trees, flowering shrubs, and annuals create a sense of mystery. Visitors catch only glimpses into adjoining rooms, which entice them to walk the flagstone path through the gateway to explore further.

The lure of the stone path welcomes guests to the living rooms—literally "living" rooms, created with a canopy of twining wisteria and climbing roses for the overhead plane and shimmering birch leaves and feathery white pines for the walls. The centerpiece of the outdoor house is the living room, where visitors catch glimpses of the other garden rooms. Comfortable seating is provided by a couch with plump, blue pillows. Water trickles around a salvaged granite millstone fountain, a tangible remnant of the historic area. From here, the dining room is visible, with its cerulean blue picnic table and hanging chandelier filled with candles. The dining room is also covered with a shade arbor, so lunches can be enjoyed in a bit of shade, even in the height of summer. To the right of the outdoor dining room is the outdoor kitchen.

Stone steps lined with verbena and blue catmint lead down into the kitchen garden from the old corn crib shed at the Barclay garden.

Each of the Barclays' four outdoor rooms—the living room, dining room, kitchen, and potager—complement each other and are designed to flow into one another. Each is an enclosed garden, a *hortus conclusus*, created from the existing and new building structures, the flowering shrubs and trees, the overhead trellises, the picket fence, and, of course, the stone wall.

An entrance leads from the potager to the Barclays' outdoor living and dining rooms. The back of the kitchen, with its stone wall and red metal roof, helps create the space of the potager garden.

The Barclay garden stone wall forms the backdrop for the outdoor living room, with a ceiling created from old timbers that includes a fan and lights for conversations with friends, day or night.

The Barclays' outdoor dining room has a flagstone floor and custom chandelier; a rustic wood fence creates the room's back wall.

The outdoor kitchen

The kitchen nook is covered with a red tin roof that complements the roof of the main house. This kitchen contains all the comforts of an indoor kitchen: a work table, stove, sink, and refrigerator—paradise for the cook who loves to garden or the gardener who loves to cook. Either way, when Gay entertains, the salad bar is actually the garden, where diners can choose from baby mesclun, baby spinach, sugar snap peas, and cherry tomatoes. Drinks are served cold from the fridge and sauces are kept hot on the stove. A stir-fry of rare mixed vegetables is harvested, quick-cooked, and eaten within minutes—all within the garden. This outdoor kitchen is connected visually to the other parts of the outdoor house by the stone wall that continues in the living and dining rooms. Behind this wall is the outdoor pantry—the potager.

The well-stocked outdoor pantry

The space of the potager is created by a stable for the ponies, which forms one wall to the south, and towering pine trees that form the northern wall. The back of the kitchen forms a wall to the west. Everything is surrounded by a whimsical and practical picket fence that keeps rabbits and other creatures from devouring the vegetables. The potting shed is the central feature of

The outdoor pantry at the Barclay garden is a formal rectilinear layout of raised beds with sculptural trellises, creating a pleasing view.

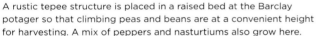
A rustic tepee structure is placed in a raised bed at the Barclay potager so that climbing peas and beans are at a convenient height for harvesting. A mix of peppers and nasturtiums also grow here.

The rose-covered arbor extends from the potting shed, the workroom of the Barclay potager, where Gay stores her tools and supplies.

this space; it was created from an old barn on the property, so it holds a memory of an earlier time on the farm. This central workstation holds well-organized tools and potting supplies. Gay's special box of collected seeds from around the world, including heirloom tomato seeds from Château de la Bourdaisière in France, is kept dry under the tin roof.

On each side of the potting shed are the raised beds, which measure 4 by 14 ft. (1 by 4 m) and are 18 in. (46 cm) high. These raised beds are an ideal width—all the vegetables, herbs, and flowers are within easy reach for harvesting and maintenance. The rustic tepee trellises in the raised beds put all the vining plants at a convenient height for harvesting—requiring not too much bending to access the vegetables. Gay grows peas and beans, morning glories, and miniature pumpkins on the sculptural structures. This living garden of edible delights is the outdoor fruitful pantry.

Gay Barclay enjoys a harvest of spring radishes, a cool-season, fast crop that is easy to grow.

One of the raised beds is fitted with hinged, clear plastic adjustable lids to form a cold frame. Gay is able to grow spinach, mustard, and other succulent greens here year-round. This is also an incubation place for starting seedlings that can be transplanted to other parts of the garden during the growing season, to fill in any holes left by harvesting. Sprawling vegetables, such as cucumbers and squash, are given ample room on the sloped hillside, near the pump fountain. 'Trombocino' squash spreads among the flowers.

A well-designed feature of the potager is the large, covered compost bin, located near the cold frame and within a shovel's throw of the raised beds. Adjacent to the bin is a wide stone ramp that leads to the upper level of the garden, near the stables. This allows Gay to push a wheelbarrow full of clippings up the ramp and dump it into the bin. Manure, a source of nutrition for building the soil, is also nearby. Finished compost is removed through sliding doors at the lower garden level, where it is most needed.

At the edge of the Barclay potager is the cold frame, where Gay nurtures new seedlings. Spinach and other cool season vegetables grow in this cold frame throughout the winter.

Lettuce is planted in neat rows in the Barclay garden. Gay adds twine to the wood trellises so that the delicate tendrils of pea vines can easily climb.

Chives form an attractive edge in a raised bed in the Barclay potager garden, which is protected on one side by tall white pines.

THE POTAGER AT NORTH HILL

The North Hill potager garden in Readsboro, Vermont (Zone 4), was designed by two talented landscape designers and garden writers who value their kitchen garden not only as a personal retreat but as the source of the bounty that supplies their table throughout the year. A quick run to the grocery store is not an option in this remote haven—rather, a peaceful walk through the woods to the kitchen garden during the growing season or to the greenhouse/storage shed in the winter provides the fresh herbs and produce for a meal.

Joe Eck and Wayne Winterrowd have lived this way, dependent on the garden and its seasons, for many years. They plant what they love to eat—often rare and precious heirloom varieties—and they plant fruits and vegetables that are beautiful to look at, lined up in neat rows and squares separated by straw pathways and espaliered fruit trees. The kitchen garden at North Hill is a rare example of the American potager: it is an enclosed edible garden that is beautifully and artfully designed to be a haven and a pantry.

The kitchen garden at North Hill has evolved over time as the owners have gained garden wisdom, with more than 30 years of practicing design and studying the land they inhabit. An intimate knowledge of the Vermont landscape and years of experience in design and growing food

A view back to the simple wooden gate through which one enters the North Hill potager. Practical growing squares and rectangles are surrounded with straw paths and punctuated with a fruit tree or bamboo tepee. (Photo by James E. Matson)

has prompted a few location changes for the kitchen garden. The current potager is a perfect balance of utility and beauty, with the best mix of location, size, and enclosure. The location, the fencing, the arrival, the gateway, and the plots themselves have been created for the pleasure of the owners and their lucky guests. This potager is an excellent example of how planning and design elevate the vegetable plot to a special place, almost a sacred destination full of meaning and beauty.

Follow the path

The mantra "Plant the kitchen garden near the kitchen" doesn't apply to the kitchen garden at North Hill. For most homes and restaurants, the close proximity of the potager to the kitchen is a practical necessity when the garden is used on a daily basis, but in certain situations, an addendum to this rule is appropriate. At North Hill, the rule is "Create a magical experience on your way to the kitchen garden." If you have the space, you can create a special journey to the kitchen garden as part of the overall design.

A simple arrangement of tools and pottery tells the story of North Hill—there is beauty in utility.

North Hill encompasses 23 acres of rolling woodland; the size of this rural estate required that the designers plan the location of the kitchen garden as a part of the design of the entire property. Although the garden has evolved over many years in its location, every element of the property is part of an overall master plan—a grand scheme of integrated elements that flow one to the other. The placement of the house, driveway, guest house, perennial garden, rose garden, shelter, poultry house, and the kitchen garden forms a series of spaces connected by pathways; not only is each garden room a special place, but the entire effect is that of a well-designed landscape.

A flat of mixed lettuces could be transplanted to fill in holes left in the potager from harvesting other vegetables, or it could be placed merely to brighten a seating area.

The kitchen garden, including the journey to it, is part of the garden experience that is North Hill. Joe and Wayne have mastered the pathway as part of the potager experience. Other trails diverge from the main path into the woods, including a fork leading down to a stream. The visitor may encounter a flat of lettuce or edible nasturtiums placed on a wooden bench on the covered plank bridge that crosses the stream, waiting to be carried to the garden for planting.

The grass path, flanked by tiger lilies, narrows at the open gate that welcomes visitors through a rough-hewn wood pergola covered with roses and flowering vines. The mulch path curves beneath the canopy of a pergola so that the view ahead is hidden and a little mysterious. The Vermont woods encroach on the pathway, and everywhere the eye alights is evidence of a designer's hand, with well-placed evergreens, alpines, ferns, and perennials blending with the native woodland. An opening leads to a meadow and the gate to the kitchen garden.

The journey to the potager at North Hill is part of the experience and therefore part of the potager. Wayne shares the experience:

> When we go up to work in the vegetable garden, it is like a little vacation—so peaceful, so controlled and contained. For that reason, until we are very old, and then have to put our vegetables back in the backyard . . . we would not have it anyplace else. That

The rustic pergola planted with native American and Asian woodland perennials helps to create the special journey along the path to the North Hill potager.

sense of distance and remoteness is quite precious to us. And the vegetable garden is perhaps the part of the whole vast garden we would give up last.

Layers of enclosure

The potager at North Hill is truly a haven carved out of the woods, so reminiscent of the Western archetype of the clearing in the forest. This garden has multiple layers of enclosure, which create the framework that conveys the feeling of oasis and separateness from the pressures of busy lives. These edges create this *hortus conclusus* in the wilderness.

The highest and most remote wall of the garden is the surrounding maple and beech forest. The three acre clearing in the woods creates a haven of light that contrasts with the dark and towering hardwood trees. The second layer of enclosure is the stone wall that was created when the meadow was cleared for growing vegetables. The hand-built wall runs the length of the garden and stands at the edge of the woods. The most evident enclosure to the 60 by 80 ft. (18 by 24 m) formal vegetable garden is the split rail locust fence, which keeps out the geese and forms a support for espaliered fruit trees and wandering pea vines. This border surrounds the garden room, setting the edge that dictates the formation of the smaller rectangular beds that create patterns in the garden. The weathered pine poultry house at

A wall of towering hardwood trees form the visual edge to the kitchen garden at North Hill.

the north edge of the garden also contributes a wall to the enclosure.

Everything grows here

In this Zone 4 paradise garden, Wayne and Joe enjoy the taste and beauty of highbush blueberries, gooseberries, red currants, pears, apples, apricots, and strawberries—which lend a permanent focal point to the garden as the fruit trees and standards are often planted at the center of a square. Numerous varieties of annual heirloom vegetables, herbs, and some flowers are planted in neat rows and squares to create a patchwork of color, taste, and fragrance.

The gardeners are undeterred by the seeming constraints of their northern climate zone and harvest a plentiful variety of heat-loving plants. Managing and amending the soil is one contributing factor to the health of the soil and therefore the garden. Aged manure from the owners' Scots Highland cows, the poultry, and the piglets—as well as a large compost bed and amendments of phosphorus—ensure that warm-season vegetables that might be borderline in this altitude and climate have the best chance for survival. Plants from the heat-loving nightshade family (tomatoes, peppers, and eggplants) are planted out only when they have grown to a healthy transplant size.

After tasting homegrown artichokes, Wayne and Joe will never go back to the store-bought variety. The native Mediterranean biennial artichokes can be grown in this climate with a fair amount of coaxing and labor. The tender delicacies are grown from seed started in winter and then transplanted into the garden in spring. 'Imperial Star' is able to set buds in one growing season, and Joe and Wayne recommend this variety for colder climates.

The locust split rail fence at North Hill provides support for the espaliered fruit trees. A kale forcing pot made by Connecticut potter Guy Wolff provides winter protection for an artichoke crown later in the year.

Just outside the split rail fence is North Hill's pig house, where two piglets reside and receive excess or overgrown produce, such as the corn, lettuce, peppers, and beans planted in neat rows in the garden.

The pig house and forest provide the backdrop to the wide-angle view of the North Hill potager. A bright yellow chair, a rusty find at a junk shop, invites a rest at the end of a row of artichokes.

Brussels sprout plants will continue to grow at North Hill even when the weather turns cool in the fall, yielding a crop for the Thanksgiving table.

At North Hill, red currants are trained to grow as standards amid the Swiss chard and onions and provide a feast for the eyes as well as the main ingredient in a sauce or jam. As currants have few surface roots, they do not compete with crops clustered around their trunks.

At North Hill, bamboo poles provide the structure for the tomato plants that will need some control later in the season, when side growths are removed and vines are trained upward to conserve space.

Fresh tomatoes with freshly gathered basil can be added to pasta for a delicious summertime lunch.

CHAPTER FOUR

Why a Garden?

ONE DAY my collegiate daughter came by with a friend to pick up something from the house. It was an impromptu visit and of course they were hungry. "What do we have to eat?" The cupboards and refrigerator doors were opened and then slammed shut to see what, if any, treasures were inside. I hesitated before speaking to gauge how hungry they really were, but the level of hunger was not really the important question. This was an unexpected homecoming. The point was to sit down, visit, enjoy each other's company, and meet her new friend. Good food is always a great way to accommodate fellowship, and memories of family holidays or religious celebrations can flood our minds when certain smells are re-created. It was the middle of an August afternoon, so we all walked out to the garden to see what was growing.

Our garden is an extension of the house, and guests are naturally drawn to this central gathering place. We entered through the garden gate, and the Williamsburg gate ball and chain immediately drew it closed behind us. I told the old family stories of how the potager came to be over the years, explaining how we hauled, piece by piece, the 2500 bricks from a collapsed building to our backyard, and how all the children (and neighbors) helped to chip concrete from the brick. This was free brick at a very high cost. Now family and friends come here to enjoy the fruits of our labor and the harvest of the garden.

We tasted the mix of red and green lettuce, tatsoi mustard greens, 'Bull's Blood' beet greens, haricot verts, calendula, and red nasturtium flowers from the central raised beds. No need to gather any more items for a salad, as we had already eaten it fresh and without dressing. As we

Tropaeolum majus 'Empress of India' nasturtium has blue-green leaves and deep orange-red flowers with a spicy, peppery flavor.

Freshly picked sweet basils (*Ocimum basilicum* 'Genovese' and *O. basilicum* 'Cinnamon'), heirloom 'Orange Banana' tomatoes (*Solanum lycopersicum* 'Orange Banana'), and bull's horn sweet peppers (*Capsicum annuum* 'Corno di Toro Rosso') make colorful additions to pasta.

watched a hummingbird enjoying the nectar from the red throat of the 'Scarlet Emperor' runner bean flower, we gathered basil leaves and flowers, Italian flat leaf parsley, heirloom sweet peppers, and heirloom tomatoes. The heirloom 'Chesnok Red' garlic cloves had already been harvested in late July and were drying in the house. These vegetables and herbs of the day would be served with pasta for a fast, impromptu snack.

A fruity aroma engulfed the kitchen as we prepared the just-picked vegetables, still warm from the August sunshine. Washing vegetables is a ritual; while no pesticides or chemicals are used on them, rinsing does remove clinging soil particles. We removed the stems from the parsley and basil. We coarsely chopped the green leaves of the herbs and added them to the olive oil, where they were allowed to go limp before we removed the pan from the heat. We added coarsely ground pepper and sea salt. When the pasta was done, it was drained and added to the hot olive oil and vegetables. We grated the hard cheese at the table. While gathering, chopping, and cooking, we covered topics from Ph.D. programs and travels in Greece to childhood memories of adventures searching for wild turtles. We sat down to enjoy a simple, flavorful, soul-satisfying meal and continue the conversation. The bountiful garden allowed us to slow down, relax, and freely share our thoughts.

How do we want to eat? The answer to this question eventually adds up to the way we live our lives. Harvesting, cooking, and eating garden-grown food is a way to connect with friends and family in a profound way. It's not just about sitting down at a nicely set table—it is the entire ritual of gathering and cooking. The aromas as the meal cooks, the feel of handmade pie crust as we roll out the dough, the sight of children eating the just-picked berries from the garden before they make it to the pie, and finally the taste of a warm piece of berry pie—these are memories our gardens impart to those we love. A well-designed kitchen garden becomes the focal point for gatherings, and the fruits, herbs, and vegetables connect us with the seasons.

RESTORATION SOUP

A restaurant is a place where meals are served to the public, but the word *restaurant* carries a deeper history and meaning. The word comes from the French verb *restaurer*, which means to restore. The original French refers to a restorative soup, so the word has significance as a place to go for restoration. Also, remember that *hortus conclusus* is an oasis and a place of refuge and *potage* is a hearty soup. Potagers are places of restoration that provide food and nourishment. A deep and mysterious relationship exists between food and having our spirits lifted, and this relationship is profoundly and ultimately tied to the garden.

Have some restaurants lost the ability to offer restorative soup? Certainly something is lost when we don't sit down to enjoy "real" food. With a growing trend toward slower living and savoring authentic food, many chefs are planting their own gardens so they have access to fresh and uncommon herbs and vegetables. In these restaurants, the organic garden is the source of artistically prepared meals that allow diners to celebrate with friends over an intimate dinner or an elaborate festive occasion.

THE RYLAND INN
A place of wonder

One of the world's finest chefs creates his menu on a daily basis depending on what is growing in his New Jersey (Zone 6) garden. This garden is part of his restaurant and the inspiration for the creative menu at The Ryland Inn in Whitehouse, New Jersey. Chef Craig Shelton has a philosophy about how food through the seasons relates to the seasons of a man's life—similar to the *Voyage of Life* paintings by Thomas Cole, but at The Ryland, the art is food. The pairings of artistic wines with each daily menu evolve as well as the fare.

Craig is connected to nature and the changing seasons and knows well how this relates to the subtle changes in intensity of flavors throughout the year. The owner and chef of The Ryland Inn is a winner of numerous culinary awards, but he is a man of many seasons: a Yale graduate with degrees in molecular biophysics and biochemistry, he has also apprenticed under some of the most renowned chefs in France. He appeared on the American

A menagerie of raised beds produces flowers, herbs, and vegetables for the restaurant table of chef Craig Shelton at The Ryland Inn in Whitehouse, New Jersey.

television series *Great Chefs of the East*, and The Ryland Inn was one of only 20 restaurants in the United States recognized by the prestigious association Relais & Châteaux as a "Relais Gourmand" restaurant. According to The Ryland Inn's website, Alice Waters, celebrated author, chef, and owner of the Bay Area's Chez Panisse restaurant, named The Ryland Inn's vegetable and herb garden "the best kitchen garden in America." Could it be that the ultimate experience of haute cuisine originates in the simplicity of the garden?

Environmental lawyer to organic gardener

Chip Shepherd used to live the life of a corporate environmental lawyer with all the perks, but he had no time to appreciate the actual environment. Now he rides his bicycle to work every day in the three acre organic garden at The Ryland Inn, where he is the garden manager. He spends his days working in paradise to ensure that it remains so. He also spends his time passionately educating others on the benefits and art of organic gardening.

Herbs, flowers, and vegetables are grown without pesticides and herbicides and are used in the kitchen and to decorate the table at The Ryland Inn.

Speaking with Chip, one cannot help but think of Mary in Frances Hodgson Burnett's *The Secret Garden* and her wonder at the miracles growing behind the garden wall. Such was the passion that woke her up every morning to run to the garden to see what had changed. Chip is also enthralled by the garden. On one morning, he was particularly excited because he had found a hidden treasure in the potager. A cold frame that had been covered and forgotten had been rediscovered. He opened the lid to find the green leaves of perfect arugula waiting to be harvested.

Chip says that every day is an adventure, watching for the first fingerling asparagus to poke through the ground or discovering an unexpected gift of several baby patty pan squash that didn't exist the day before. This enthusiasm is shared by the chefs as they frequently venture to the garden to see the precious daily surprises.

Chip encourages guests in his organic gardening classes to spend time every day in their own gardens and pay attention. He advises gardeners to check their gardens in the morning and evening, and if possible during the day. The faithful observer will not only see the mysteries of growth but will be able to detect how plants are faring; wilted, infected plants can be removed immediately before more damage occurs. The gardener can make notes as to what plants do well in specific places. Chip, a master of detail, finds ideal placement for his plants in the garden, focusing on particular microclimates and their suitability to particular plants' needs.

The Ryland Inn garden models nature: diversity and variety are the mandate. The art of companion planting means that herbs, flowers, and

Ornamental corn is grown for floral arrangements at The Ryland Inn. Although it does not produce edible fruit, the plant attracts beneficial insects to the organic garden.

Blue hyssop (*Hyssopus officinalis*) grows abundantly in the organic garden at The Ryland Inn, attracting bees and hummingbirds; it can be dried for tea or used in arrangements.

vegetables are often planted in the same row, but no rigid partnership dictates that "carrots should always be planted with dill" and so forth. Chip considers the garden a giant experiment.

Jardin potager

The three acre garden produces a wide variety of herbs, edible flowers, vegetables, and fruits. The flowers serve two purposes: edible flowers are served in the restaurant, and the homegrown bouquets are used to decorate the inn. The emphasis is on variety, and each edible plant becomes a delicacy.

Craig adjusts the menu daily, based on what is growing in the garden. This is truly the philosophy of the *jardin potager*. He believes that it is more important to serve special fresh ingredients for a few days or weeks than to produce one item throughout the growing season. Because of the garden, Craig is able to use ingredients in his dishes that he would be unable to procure otherwise. One spring day, as Chip was thinning the celeriac plants, a few lucky guests received these fragile delicacies on their salads. This edible treat was "planned" by the garden, not by the chef. Another day, fragile microgreens and baby lettuces were picked from the garden only moments before they were presented on the plate, and artichokes were harvested and cooked within minutes of serving.

Garden visit

The Ryland Inn garden is hidden from view but is located a short walk from the restaurant through a grassy field. A well-worn path leads from the back door of the kitchen to the gateway of the potager. Chefs take this path many times a day to gather the freshest ingredients. The garden is also open to patrons, and Chip says the experience of eating in the restaurant is enhanced if diners stroll through the garden before sitting down to enjoy the meal.

An abundance of diverse plants from elderberries to coneflowers ensures that something is always in season at The Ryland Inn.

Poppies have almost finished flowering while blue-green onions await harvest, contrasting with the golden yellow portulaca in the kitchen garden at The Ryland Inn.

Spiky artichokes grown at The Ryland Inn potager can be gathered when they are small and tender and will be on the table within minutes of harvest.

Hop vines (*Humulus lupulus*) grow to 14 ft. (4 m) in the garden at The Ryland Inn and produce hops for homemade beer; the plant also produces edible shoots.

This expansive garden welcomes guests through the gate with grape vines overhanging a wooden trellis. The garden is divided into sections, but the original section is the herb garden, with raised beds and a grand variety of planted herbs. Numerous varieties of purple and green basils are mixed in, and the chefs appreciate the shiso (*Perilla frutescens* var. *purpurascens*) that seeds itself and appears in various spots in the garden over the years.

The Ryland Inn's sous chef checks the garden daily to help Craig prepare the menu. This garden has such variety that something is always ready to be harvested—this is the goal, says Chip. It is not a static process of planting the garden in the spring and harvesting in the fall. This garden is an ongoing, evolving process. Half of the beds will be planted with two or more crops throughout the growing season; after one crop has been harvested, the beds are planted with a crop of new vegetables appropriate for the season.

What's on the menu?

What is growing in the garden is served at the table. Daily, throughout June, haricot verts and baby patty pan squash are harvested; what remains on the

A cluster of organically grown grapes overhangs the entrance gate to the garden at The Ryland Inn.

Purple and green basil varieties are easy to grow and create a striking display of contrast and color in The Ryland Inn potager.

A variety of squash and haricot verts have been harvested from The Ryland Inn garden for the evening menu.

plants are the next day's dinner ingredients. The tasting menus, offering traditional, gourmet, and vegetarian choices, allow patrons to sample a seven-course meal with selected wine pairings if desired. For example, baby leeks and potatoes are picked fresh from the garden to create a vichyssoise with black truffle ice cream, served in a clear bowl with another bowl of ice underneath to keep the soup at its perfect serving temperature. This chilled soup has three distinct layers: the crusty top layer, the creamy soup layer, and the black truffle ice cream layer. Minutes before the dinner hour, the sous chef walks through the garden, selecting the vegetables to be fried in the Japanese manner, including crispy shiso leaves with serrated edges and deep purple color. This tempura of organic garden vegetables is served with nori salt and white soy sauce. Heirloom tomatoes in the tomato confiture are slowly oven roasted to a thick, sweet consistency, almost like tomato jam.

Servers educate diners about each course—how the meat, seafood, and vegetables are prepared. The *sommelier* tells diners how the wine is selected for each pairing. Heady and elegant progressions and deepening flavors throughout the evening make the entire experience one fluid memory, but diners also remember each individual creation and how each course complements or contrasts with another. These flavors result from fresh, organic ingredients.

Dependent on nature

Chip's role as garden manager means that he ensures a bountiful harvest of delicacies for the chefs, and he intervenes when things go wrong. Looking over the yellow squash blossoms, he may notice some striped beetles enjoying the flowers—unwelcome visitors that can spread disease throughout the plants. After hand picking the beetles off the plants, he sprays with an organic powder to coat the plants; the garden has been designated "certified organic" by the Northeast Organic Farming Association (NOFA), and no pesticides or herbicides are used. In the end, sometimes nature wins, but Chip is relaxed and calm as he observes this fact. He knows that growing produce is a humble adventure that is often out of our control but always rewards us with new experiences.

Shiso, or red perilla (*Perilla frutescens* var. *purpurascens*) is used in Japanese cooking and found in various parts of the garden at The Ryland Inn.

Fresh patty pan squash harvested in the morning will appear on evening dinner plates at The Ryland Inn.

DRAGONFLY NEO-V CUISINE
A garden as a symbol of healing and choice

For Magdiale Wolmark and Cristin Austin, changing the world begins at home. Their current home is Dragonfly Neo-V Cuisine, which has been listed as one of the top 10 restaurants in Columbus, Ohio, by *The Columbus Dispatch* and one of the 10 best vegetarian restaurants in the nation by *USA Today*. Here in a trendy spot in historic Victorian Village near The Ohio State University, they are living the ultimate connected life, where their passion is their profession and their home is where they work, play, and invite the neighborhood over for dinner. Magdiale is the visionary chef, determined to change people's minds about the taste of vegan food. Here, diners find fabulous vegetarian cuisine that even meat-lovers enjoy.

Rise up, dig in, go local

While diners enjoy such entréees as "Butternut squash gnocchi with dried tomatoes, mantequilla olives, grilled portobello with a confit of garlic, capers, and lemon coconut milk cream" from the seasonally changing menu, they are assured that all the fare is organically grown. The chef has developed relationships with nearby farmers so that whenever possible the food has been grown in central Ohio, a few miles down the road from the restaurant. Diners enjoy the bounty of the small-scale organic local farmer and local artisans who have put together a restaurant that surrounds them with beauty. This is good for the community; it supports the small, family-owned farms and preserves a precious shrinking resource. Dragonfly's battle cry is "Rise up, dig in, go local."

Small garden, big ideas

Expansive thinking has led to the creation of the restaurant's outdoor garden, where the coveted chef's table is in the center, just outside the glass kitchen door. Patrons are surrounded by the beauty of growing vegetables, herbs, and flowers and get to peek into the source of the creation of the artistic food, the Dragonfly kitchen. The garden is intended for the community, and Magdiale has always envisioned it to be so. He is working with the city to allow the alley adjacent to the restaurant to be used only as a pedestrian way so neighborhood children can safely walk to the garden for lessons on growing, harvesting, cooking, and eating fresh delicacies such as jostaberries and bright yellow, edible calendula flowers. The kitchen garden at Dragonfly Neo-V Cuisine is a partnership with the Greater Columbus

Foodshed Project, an organization committed to helping promote urban community gardens.

This small garden sits on a small lot in an urban neighborhood. In no way will the herbs and vegetables produced here supply the kitchen with all it needs on a daily basis; Magdiale has local farmers for that. The garden here is a symbol of the importance of the purity of food—a reminder that luscious, fruitful, climbing vines and tiny green sprouts are not only the source of great cuisine but also of creativity and healing.

DESIGN THE POTAGER AS PART OF YOUR HOME

These award-winning chefs are now cultivating their own potager gardens or buying from growers who grow unusual heirloom vegetables in addition to the wide range of commonly used herbs for seasoning and garnishes. Although this demand for fresh produce is growing, what is still lacking is a simple way for the chef or home cook to establish the kitchen garden. If the goal is fresh produce, why not place the garden literally next to the kitchen? Better yet, why not make the beautiful vegetable, fruit, herb, and flower garden a part of the dining experience?

We can plant cultivated berry varieties in our own gardens so that our children learn to taste a sun-ripened raspberry from the prickly bush. We can create our potager as part of our home—a connection between the indoor kitchen and the outdoor garden, where we daily enjoy the beauty and bounty of the visual, sensual, edible delights. This is the American potager, where the beauty and the bounty of the garden are reunited, enriching our daily lives.

A delightful presentation of organic vegan cuisine is the specialty at Dragonfly Neo-V Cuisine in Columbus, Ohio. (Photo by Mark Cheadle)

A simple high-backed bench creates an edge to Corrine Yager's potager and provides a resting place for visitors to enjoy the quietness of the garden.

CHAPTER FIVE

Design Principles of the Modern Potager

THE POTAGER is to be used and enjoyed year-round to stock the soup pot with food harvested during the changing seasons. From baby asparagus soup in the spring to hearty pumpkin soup in the fall, what we serve at the table depends on what is growing in the garden. Throughout the growing and harvest season, when flowers, fruits, herbs, and vegetables flourish and grow, we can visit the garden many times daily to observe the changes that can occur almost hourly. If the zucchini has reached the perfect fingerling size, it must be harvested while it is tender, for tomorrow the squash will bloat and be destined only for bread—way too much zucchini bread.

Since we are using the garden daily to harvest and eat the best-tasting produce, we must view the garden in a way that differs from the typical American vegetable garden, stuck in the far corner of the backyard as an afterthought. The potager garden should be as elegant as the specialty food that is grown there. It should be designed like a favorite room and feel like a favorite chair—comfortable, relaxing, and inviting. It is a place to which we are drawn for spiritual restoration as well as for the food it provides.

By applying basic principles of design, we can decorate the garden room as we might any room in our house. The word *decorate* should be used very carefully: We should not think of placing items superficially throughout the garden as we might randomly hang pictures on a wall. Rather, we should consider the space and framework of the garden—how we want to feel in the garden, where we want to build the garden, and where the potager begins and ends.

To begin the discussion of creating a special place for growing edible plants, it is helpful to view your property as a garden first and foremost.

BEGIN WITH AN ACCURATE MAP

The first step in the garden design process is to know and understand the existing conditions on your property. A site analysis will allow you to create a framework for designing the garden; know the positive aspects as well as the constraints of the site. Begin by creating a map of your property—it doesn't have to be a complicated rendered drawing, but it should be accurate.

You can create an accurate map in a number of ways. The least expensive way is to take your own measurements and then translate them to some graph paper. Before you begin, you may want to purchase an architect's scale that allows you to draw your map to a given scale. For example, with an ⅛ in. architect's scale, ⅛ in. = 1 ft.—that is, 1 inch on your paper reflects 8 feet in reality.

Another way to obtain a map is to purchase a copy of an aerial view or CAD (computer aided design) drawing of your property, which can be printed for you at your local county auditor's office. Many counties in the United States make this available for a fee. For a typical suburban or urban lot, printing the plan at ⅛ in. scale is a convenient working scale. The aerial view will be printed typically with north at the top of the page.

After you have purchased or drawn your map, you can draw in or locate your house or restaurant, other existing buildings such as garages or sheds, driveways, walkways, patios, fences, and existing large trees. Make note of structures on neighboring properties, as sometimes they impact your property—a neighbor's mature tree or existing shed may create shade across your property, or it may be unsightly and you want to block the view, or it may be a fabulous view that you can "borrow" so you can see it from your garden.

After you have created a general base plan of your site, purchase a roll of tracing paper from an art store and roll it out over the base map; you can sketch ideas directly on the tracing paper rather than on your map. Keep the base map unmarked as a permanent example of existing conditions and structures. Grab some colorful markers and begin to color in the design with a few principles in mind.

PRINCIPLE ONE
Consider technicalities

First consider practical matters of sun and shade. Ideally, the garden should be placed in a location where it can receive at least six hours of sunlight per day. Most vegetables require full sun to thrive; the more sun, the greater the health of most plants. Remember that the sun will be higher in the sky during the summer, so the long shadows of winter will not give you an accurate snapshot of the summer garden.

Aspect of the garden is also important. Where will the potager be located relative to the house and kitchen? If the building faces south, east, or west, a potager that you enter and pass through on your way to the front door will make for a pleasant and fragrant arrival. If the rear of the house faces south, east, or west, the kitchen garden should be incorporated into the design of the available private backyard space. What about a northern exposure? The north side of buildings and structures will always be in some shadow. The simple truth is that a garden planted on the north side of a building will not receive enough sun to grow many vegetables.

Nevertheless, full sun is not always possible, especially in urban spaces or in older neighborhoods with large shade trees. Shade will limit the vegetables you can grow, but a shady potager is possible. Many herbs such as parsley and a variety of greens prefer some shade. Even if you are limited in your availability of full sun, you can experiment with the possibilities.

PRINCIPLE TWO
Maximize the kitchen–garden relationship

The second principle in creating the potager is to plant the garden near the kitchen so the chef has easy access to the dill for the poached salmon and the tomatillos, cilantro, and garlic for the salsa. A kitchen garden that is close to the kitchen is easy to use, even on rainy days, when the parsley and oregano are just a quick step out the back door.

Another reason to place the kitchen garden near the kitchen is equally important: the garden is near the house because it is an extension of the house. The interior of the house can flow to the outside potager by extending the use of a similar color and repeating a material—for example, stone pavers in the kitchen can extend through the doorway and into the garden. Likewise, the garden seems to flow into the house: as windows and glass doors bring plant views into the house, the outside comes in.

Place the garden next to the house in a prominent location, so windows in the family room, living room, or kitchen overlook the garden. The potager should be beautiful to look at and a pleasure to experience, even if a vegetable is never harvested. When the weather is chilly or rainy, we can still enjoy the garden as we gaze out the window. In winter, when nothing is growing outside, the green boxwood, remaining structures, and sculptural glass cloches create a pleasant scene from inside the house.

My potager is just outside my kitchen window, where I can watch the hummingbirds sipping nectar and keep an eye on the growing herbs and vegetables.

Imagine standing at the kitchen sink by a window overlooking the splendor of the potager. You can keep an eye on the progress of the garden from the kitchen and watch as the first sprouts of lettuce appear or the early tomatoes transition to ripe red, orange, yellow, or purple. The well-stocked potager is one of the finest tools available to the cook. Consider its design when you consider the design of the kitchen.

In large estate gardens or rural gardens, locating a potager in proximity to the kitchen may not be possible. The overall master plan of the property should nevertheless make sure that the potager is part of the design of the entire landscape. For large properties with potagers located away from the house or kitchen, you can create an experience on the way to the potager. Design an enjoyable pathway that meanders with a sense of expectancy and mystery as you wind your way to the potager destination. (Recall the potager at North Hill in Chapter 3.)

PRINCIPLE THREE
Consider the bird's eye view

The French embraced the idea of the potager as part of the design and layout of the *château*. In the early *château* (which literally means a house fortress), the kitchen garden was contained within a wall in a pleasing manner, and it could be seen from the upper stories of the living quarters. During the Renaissance, the parterre garden was designed to be viewed and enjoyed from above. Eventually, intricate patterns were developed on the ground plane to be enjoyed for their elaborate detail and color. The potager, like the parterre garden, can be a piece of living artwork.

Consider the bird's eye view when designing the garden; this view into my potager is from my home's upstairs windows.

If the potager is incorporated into the design of the backyard and is near the house, the home's upper floors can look down onto the garden. This principal applies to urban gardens as well as suburban schemes. The urban potager can become an oasis in the midst of the city—a little park with fragrance and food. The Blue Steel potager, featured in Chapter 7, was designed for an urban restaurant. It is visible from a multistory office building adjacent to the garden, where office workers can look out their windows and enjoy the patterns created from the varied textures and colors in the potager. The design creates a refreshing, healing green space, even if it can't be touched from the office cubicle.

Potager layout

When designing the plan of the garden, think of dividing it into units or modules. Drawing the plan with blocks of color helps you visualize the massing of the plants. Grouping some plants together in blocks instead of planting individually helps in the crop rotation plan as well. Create the modules in a dimension that is convenient for the beds—the typical arm's reach is about 2 ft. (61 cm); double that, and you have a total bed width dimension of about 4 ft. (1 m). This is how far most of us can reach when weeding and maintaining the beds without walking on and compacting the soil.

Using rectilinear forms in the garden layout is a natural result of using the rectilinear forms for the raised beds. Create several repetitive modular beds with pathways in between. You can use a grid layout even in the suburban garden. We are so often influenced by the ubiquitous curvilinear layout featured in residential design that we think we have no other options, but a strong, ordered, rectilinear layout for a kitchen garden can be a powerful and bold design statement in any landscape.

The pathways between the beds are important to consider when laying out the plan. The scale and width of the pathways should relate to the size of the garden. A small, urban, private garden could feature narrow walkways between the beds. A public garden requires a wider pedestrian pathway, and in such a situation, 10 ft. (3 m) or more space between beds would be appropriate. Three feet (1 m) is a comfortable width for a gardener to move a wheelbarrow through the garden for cleanup of the beds or for adding compost, and that is an appropriate width for most residential potagers.

Répétez, s'il vous plaît

Simple rectilinear beds are repeated throughout my potager, where tomatoes, runner beans, basil, and cabbage share a bed with lavender.

Repeating colors, materials, and structures is a simple way to create unity. Repetition can be used to create a pleasing overall design: the same type of plants can be used multiple times to create a unity in color or texture,

My friend Sara enjoys the solitude of a fall evening while planting bulbs of garlic within the enclosure of my garden. (Photo by Melissa Tetirick)

and structured planting beds can be repeated to create the design of the potager. (Recall the garden at Bois Richeux from Chapter 2, in which the planting beds were repeated for a checkerboard effect.) One square bed can become four with crossing walkways between, or four beds can become sixteen.

A consistent use of materials throughout the garden also helps unify the design. For example, granite block lining multiple beds in the potager will link the garden beds. Using the same pavement material throughout the potager also serves to unify the garden design.

PRINCIPLE FOUR
Enclose the garden

The plan view is important when we lay out a garden; it makes it easy to count and locate plants. But garden design is more than laying out plants and pavement on the ground plane. This singular viewpoint can cause us to forget that the garden has a vertical orientation—height—as well as a horizontal one—length and depth. The garden must be designed with volume in mind.

The concept of a garden as an outdoor room is an ancient one, as the *hortus conclusus* was an outdoor room open to the sky. The boundary to the garden must therefore be clear. Medieval gardens were enclosed by a wattle fence; the cloister garth of the monastery garden was enclosed by the

At the Yager potager, the open gate creates a welcome door to the visitor, but the wire fencing keeps the rabbits out.

Urban potager enclosures

Look again at the early rendering of the monastery in Turin from Chapter 1. This drawing shows a compact city with walls used to create garden rooms. The image of walled, fruitful gardens surrounded by buildings is an ideal, even for modern times.

In many sprawling cities, unused spaces can be re-created as wonderful inner-city gardens. In Columbus, Ohio, as in many American cities, many unused "between" spaces exist; these holes in the fabric of the city could be filled with green spaces—edible gardens for the community or for restaurant use. American sprawl is not limited to the Midwest, and the urban potager concept can be applied to any unused or underused space in the expanded city, not just in the central business district. Obviously, in large, metropolitan downtown districts you won't find available space adjacent to the skyscrapers; in this case, the garden can go on the roof—enclosed within a fence or wall.

surrounding buildings; the space of the *château* gardens was enclosed by the wall of the *château*; the Renaissance potager was enclosed by a stone wall built around the garden. The modern lesson is this: Enclose the garden to create a special place. The enclosure creates the separation between the hectic outside world and the sanctuary of the potager.

Use existing walls

In urban and suburban areas, existing buildings adjacent to the garden can form the potager walls. An additional fence or wall may not be needed if existing buildings or part of your house can be used as part of the boundary wall of your potager. You can extend the boundary line with a fence or stone wall to extend the enclosure. Adding structures such as a potting shed or small greenhouse can also contribute to the enclosure and be incorporated into the overall design.

Walls and fences serve practical purposes as well as design purposes. In some areas, the garden must be enclosed to keep animals out. Rabbits can devastate a sprouting kitchen garden, and barrier fencing helps to keep them at bay. (But even then—well, don't forget to shut the gate.) To secure a wood fence from rabbits, a roll of wire fencing a few feet high can be stapled to the wood on the outside of the fence. Surround the entire garden with the wire fencing, ensuring that it extends below the soil a few inches. Attached to a wood fence, the wire fence is fairly invisible—except to the rabbits.

PRINCIPLE FIVE
Design the garden room's texture, color, and mood

The potager that becomes part of the residential landscape should incorporate the materials and colors used throughout the outdoor design. Although the potager is its own special place with its own character, like a designed room inside the house, it may use colors from adjoining rooms in its design. When looking for design inspiration in selecting colors and materials for the potager, look first to your residence or existing buildings. A building's stone or brick façade could be repeated in the walls or walkways of the potager. Pavement material used in patios and walkways near the house could be repeated in the potager.

Designing walls

The beautiful old stone walls surrounding the potagers in France were 12 ft. (3 m) high and served functional as well as aesthetic purposes. It may not be possible (or advisable, or even legal) to build a 12 ft. stone wall around your property to create your kitchen garden, but you can still convey a sense of enclosure and accomplish the goal of forming a separate space. Stone, brick, concrete block, wood, metal, wrought iron, edible hedges—the possibilities in design and material are numerous. Consider the height of the wall or fence; every property varies in size and need. Some gardens may need a privacy fence along the property line to separate and protect the garden. This dictates a height that is higher than eye level—at least 6 ft. (2 m).

A brick or stone wall is one of the more permanent and expensive solutions available for creating a boundary in the garden. This material provides a sense of age, conveying a mood of antiquity and reminding us of farmers in early New England, who picked out stones to plow the land and marked boundaries with the ubiquitous material, just as their forefathers had done in Great Britain. If the topography is rolling or sloping, stone can be used to retain soil to allow a change in grade, and the enclosed garden becomes a sunken garden.

Consider the varieties of stone that are indigenous and therefore plentiful in your area. Granite boulders are common in the eastern United States; limestone is abundant in the Midwest; stacked walls of desert sandstone would work in the Southwest. Each type of stone varies in its color, texture, and effect. Choose a stone that you like—the wall itself is a design element, a part of the whole that creates the potager. Plant espaliered fruit trees along the sunny face of the wall where the fruit will receive the reflected heat.

Espaliered fruit trees grow well on the sunny face of a stone wall, where they receive reflected warmth.

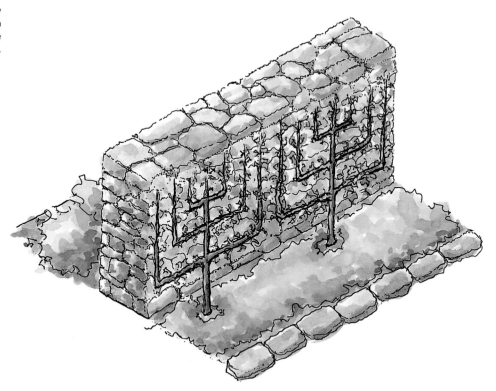

Stone and brick make excellent materials for creating a permanent seat-wall, a low wall of a comfortable height for sitting—about 18 in. (46 cm), the height of a typical dining room chair. The width of the low wall should also be comfortable for sitting. Eighteen inches to 2 ft. (46 to 61 cm) is a sufficient width, depending on the context of the garden. A substantially wider wall in the countryside would be appropriate, but a narrow wall would fit a small urban garden. A low wall creates a boundary to the kitchen garden but does not block the views from or into the garden.

The styles available in wood fencing are abundant, and wood is an economical way to enclose the potager—from a rustic split rail with an informal country look to a formal painted board privacy fence. Consider the fact that wood will require yearly maintenance—either painting or waterproofing is necessary on an ongoing basis. Picket fences can be customized for a unique look, painted or left unstained to weather to a light gray.

A simple white picket fence evokes images of a charming New England country life. This traditional fence creates a quaint kitchen or cottage garden, but classic doesn't have to be boring. Consider painting the fence

Wood picket fencing is another option for the potager wall.

a vibrant color. You'll find tremendous variety in the pickets themselves: gothic, pointed, rounded, square, and ornate. The spacing and variety in height of the pickets can also add interest.

Ornamental wrought-iron fencing is a more permanent and expensive option but ideal for a small urban garden. Depending on the scrollwork and design, this fence evokes Victorian or French influences. Unless the fence is layered with large plant material, it does not create an opaque wall but rather a transparent one. Although the garden's boundary is defined, the enclosure creates a more open feeling.

You can also consider a living wall when creating the enclosure of the kitchen garden. When planted closely together in a row, deciduous or evergreen shrubs can be used to create a permanent fence that will grow with time. The hedge height is a design decision—if the desired effect is for privacy and you have the room, a towering hornbeam hedge might be appropriate. Evaluate the plant selection based on the mature growth height of the plant. An edible wall could yield a variety of berries or hips for a complete themed garden. A well-placed group of trees or shrubs will also create a visual screen for the edible garden.

Evergreen or deciduous shrubs planted closely together create a living wall.

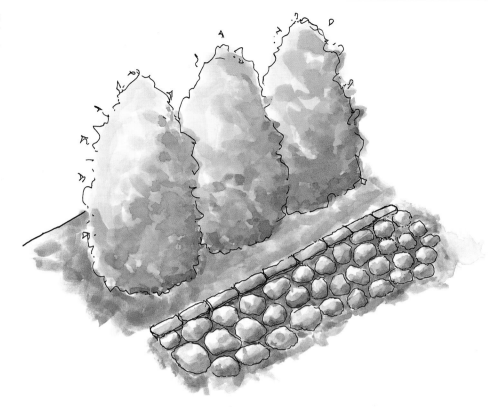

Clematis creates a green wall at one end of the garden, behind a row of bush beans.

For variety and interest, consider layering walls and plants, which provides many opportunities for a unique potager garden. A row of berry bushes planted behind a wooden picket or wrought iron fence creates more privacy. A low seat-wall with dwarf fruit trees planted behind it creates the feeling of a much taller enclosure than just the height of the wall. A 5 or 6 ft. (1.5 to 2.0 m) stone or brick wall is the perfect backdrop for a mixed perennial garden on the back side of the fence and a mixed vegetable garden on the inside of the wall.

Adding a doorway

An important feature of the potager room is the doorway into the garden. A gate creates the garden's first impression, and its impact can be increased through bold color and striking, exuberant plants or minimized as an unobtrusive pass-through. This is the spot in which to place fragrant plants to invite guests into the special garden.

One entry from the house into the enclosed garden suggests a private enclosed garden. If the potager is on the side of a house and is used to pass through from front to back, the hallway garden should have at least two entrances into the surrounding landscape.

The gate designates the entrance to a special place—my potager.

Laying the floor

When choosing the material for the garden's ground plane, consider the location and mood of the garden. In a rural, private, informal garden, the raised beds could be earth that has been mounded in rows or squares with

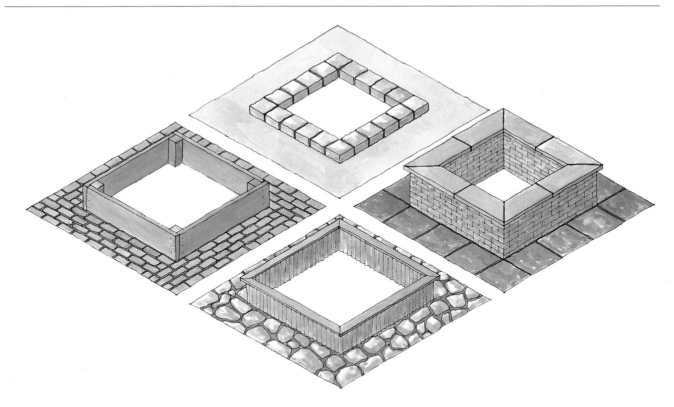

Choosing pavement and edging materials creates a special potager garden: brick with wood, crushed limestone and granite bricks, bluestone pavement with a seat-wall of brick with a stone cap, or flagstone pavement with corrugated metal edging (lined with plastic) with a wood cap.

straw pathways. The straw delineates the direction of foot traffic and protects the garden soil from compaction. This system allows the most flexibility for change from year to year. The blocks of plants, and therefore the layout design of the pathways, may be circular one year and rectilinear the next. At the end of the growing season, the weed-free straw on the pathways can be gathered and placed over the beds to protect the soil from winter erosion. Wood chips or pine needle mulch pathways are also inexpensive and allow for yearly changes in the design. This flexible system of raking and moving soil yearly is a labor-intensive choice but an inexpensive one. Grass pathways between beds are another informal option.

Numerous choices are available for pavement for permanent walkways in the kitchen garden. In a formal or public setting, where the pathways receive substantial foot traffic, a hardscape material such as brick, tile, stone, or compacted crushed gravel is perfect. Brick conveys warmth and can be rustic or formal, depending on the pattern and brick selected. Brick can be laid in a running bond, herringbone, or basket weave pattern. The patterns of stone are equally numerous: A flagstone path with irregular stones creates an informal feeling. Cut bluestone laid in a geometric pattern is more formal. Tumbled pavers have the look of old stone without the high price tag.

PRINCIPLE SIX
Create an edge with raised beds

Early medieval gardens contained raised beds in rows behind a wall or wattle fence, but raised beds in modern gardens are sensible choices as well. Raised beds allow the soil to drain easily, especially when gardening in an area with compacted clay soil. Soil is built from the top down, and rich soil can be added to the bed and replenished with compost. Raised beds warm up quickly in the spring, enabling earlier planting of some crops.

When building raised beds, consider the height of the bed. About 18 in. (46 cm) is a good height for sitting if the bed's edging material is substantial, such as stone or brick. Raising the beds to this height also puts the vegetables within easy reach. The choices in materials for the raised beds are as numerous as the choices for the pavement. Wood, rustic logs, stone, brick, concrete, and even metal are all options. Wood is one of the least expensive solutions, but make sure that you use boards that have not been treated with chromium, arsenic, or copper. All pressure-treated lumber contains these chemicals, which may leach into the surrounding soil. Better to use rot-resistant, untreated wood such as cedar. All untreated wood will need to be replaced every five years or so, as it will decay. Never use creosote-covered railroad ties or telephone poles. Galvanized metal edging should be lined with plastic to prevent leaching of chemicals.

'Bambino' hybrid eggplant is planted along the edge of the wooden border; it stays diminutive and is perfect for the edge of the bed.

Raised beds allow you to place plants close together; young basil plants will fill up the space as they grow.

PRINCIPLE SEVEN
Design for the counterpoint

Counterpoint in music occurs when two separate melodies exist at the same time. Counterpoint in garden design involves using contrasting elements, or themes, to create an overall balanced effect. Counterpoint adds interest and excitement to the kitchen garden. For example, you can use one form or color and then punctuate it with its exact opposite on the color wheel.

Chaos versus control

The dilemma in potager design is to create a balance between order and chaos. The layout of the beds forms the structural order for the garden, while the sprawling, climbing, living plants provide the chaotic counterpoint (perhaps ordered chaos). Using layers in the garden accomplishes this. The first layer is the rigid, rectilinear structure of the beds—squares, rectangles, and the sharp edges of the beds create the underlying form. The next layer is the plants—vegetables and flowers vary in height and texture, sometimes sprawling over the edge of the bed, blurring the hard lines. Plant a variety of shapes and allow them to grow exuberantly without trimming for this varying effect.

Play with the idea of the opposite, and reverse this pattern. The underlying form of the beds could be curvilinear and flowing. The edges of the beds could be created with stones or bricks in circles and arcs. The counterpoint is the plant layer—plants selected for their uniformity, laid out in neat rows and lines and kept sheared to a similar height.

The wooden raised bed is straight and rectilinear, and the plants become the counterpoint, flowing over edges and creating a chaotic exuberance. Bright orange calendula contrasts directly with the blue tepee poles to add vibrant contrast in my potager.

Purple-leaved hyacinth bean completely fills the bamboo tepee in the background, while 'Emerite' pole beans (*Phaseolus vulgaris* 'Emerite') climb the poles in the foreground. The vertical poles contrast with the flat plane of the other vegetables, and the blue colors contrast with the yellow flowers spaced throughout the garden.

'Emerite' pole beans produce lavender blossoms and then sweet, tender beans that are best picked when young and slim; note how the red nasturtiums in the background show off their color.

Color opposites, or complements

On the color wheel, red is opposite green, orange is opposite blue, and yellow is opposite purple. Use the color wheel to choose color opposites, or complements, in the garden; this is an easy way to add excitement and energy to the space. Use a predominance of one color and add accents of its complementary color. Contrasting colors placed next to each other in the garden can be pleasing to the eye—for example, plant red and green basils in alternating rows. Or plant primarily blue flowers throughout the garden, and complement them with spots of bright orange calendula.

Counterpoint is a way to have fun with design. On the tracing paper placed over the map of your property, use one color to sketch out the

'Heavenly Blue' morning glory (*Ipomoea tricolor* 'Heavenly Blue') climbs the painted poles to add verticality in the summer garden.

rectilinear grid of the structures and then overlay playful shapes of color to represent the plants. This is how professional landscape designers create exciting color schemes in their gardens.

PRINCIPLE EIGHT
Go vertical

Structures in the garden do more than support climbing vines; they are design features that punctuate the often flat, level landscape of the kitchen garden with color and sculptural whimsy. Bamboo poles can easily be lashed together into tepees to add needed height. Paint them to add individuality and more color to the garden. Pyramids and obelisks or unique structures of metal or wood can become vertical art pieces for trailing snow peas and green bean vines. These permanent structures can also add interest to the winter garden.

PRINCIPLE NINE
Consider winter use

The potager should be designed with four seasons of use in mind, even if vegetables are not harvested all year long. This is especially true if the garden is near the house, where it can be enjoyed visually throughout the seasons. In Ohio, only a greenhouse will preserve tender perennials such as rosemary, santolina, and some varieties of thyme through the winter. The heat-loving tropical basils and peppers are instantly killed with the first mildest frost. Purple and green cabbage and kale, colorful chard, brussels sprouts, and some mustards will hold their color long into the winter. Green tips of garlic will grow though the winter snow as the bulbs continue to expand underground.

A pyramidal glass cloche will not preserve rosemary through the winter in the Midwest, but it will extend the herb's life a bit—and the cloche adds beauty to the winter garden.

The potager can be designed to look good in winter; a fence and a lavender border provide structure to the garden even when plants aren't green and growing.

Boxwood along the fence in my potager provides a sense of enclosure, even in the snowy days of winter.

Shoots of heirloom garlic survive even in the Ohio winter. Clip some green winter sprigs to use like chives, wait till spring to harvest garlic "onions," or wait until summer to harvest the full-sized bulbs.

When the garden has been cleared of debris in the late fall or early winter, you can create pots of dried arrangements in the beds. In the center of the four raised beds in my potager, where the blue tepees held the climbing beans in the summer, four metal pots hold branches of red twig dogwood and sun-bleached wood. Boughs of evergreens are added for the winter holidays. These casual but pleasant arrangements bring cheery outside views into the warm kitchen.

Evergreens such as boxwood and taxus, fences, and walls hold the structural interest in the winter. Winter is a time of rest for my Zone 5 garden, but the muted colors still hold a stark beauty. Lavender turns a purple-gray and remains attractive throughout the year—this plant is irreplaceable in my garden. Winter days of light are few, and most days are short, often cloudy, and wet; this is the perfect time for dreaming and planning the new kitchen garden for the coming spring.

Gray lavender, red brick, and red twigs are the colors of winter in my potager.

Four planters filled with red twig dogwood and other branches are placed in each of the raised beds for an informal winter arrangement, as the lavender fades to a soft purple-gray.

CHAPTER SIX

Plant Combinations for Design and Sequence

TREES, SHRUBS, FLOWERS, AND VINES are all combined and arranged by the landscape designer to create an outdoor room. These changing elements create an outdoor space that is sensual and ephemeral, that connects us with nature and awakens our senses. Plant combinations create fragrances and colors that are subject to the nuances of shifting wind and light. Only plants can cause a garden room to shift and evolve in color and form through the season and through the years so that, almost miraculously, the garden we plant today will not be the same tomorrow.

The edible garden is filled with vegetables, herbs, fruits, and flowers that vary in color, form, and texture. Plant your potager because you love the taste of homegrown organic heirloom vegetables and because the leaves, stems, blossoms, vegetables, and fruits are beautiful to see, touch, and smell. The flowers on a climbing scarlet runner bean are a vibrant orange-red and contrast with a complementary color as it rests against the deep green of leafy vines. Bright yellow calendula flowers stand out against dark purple leaves of a hyacinth bean climbing a trellis. Consider the variety among the edible plants and treat them in your potager as you would flowers and shrubs in the landscape, mixing and arranging based on texture, color, fragrance, height, depth, and how the plants complement the entire picture.

Nasturtiums (*Tropaeolum majus* 'Empress of India'), globe amaranth (*Gomphrena haageana* 'Strawberry Fields'), and white zinnia (*Zinnia hybrida* 'Profusion White') border the vegetables in a community garden in Granville, Ohio.

The orange-red flowers of the 'Scarlet Emperor' runner bean climbing up bright blue poles creates a striking and colorful picture.

FOLIAGE AND TEXTURE

Vegetables from the mustard family, Brassicaceae, including kale, broccoli, and brussels sprouts, usually have large, bold leaves. 'Nero di Toscana' kale produces crinkled, dark green narrow leaves, with an upright form reminiscent of a palm (hence its common name, black palm). Sea kale, sea holly, rhubarb, artichokes, and cardoons are all perennials with striking foliage. Mass plantings of these plants become dominant sculptures in the landscape. Planted individually, they can form an exclamation point at the end of a row. They also fit well at the back of a vegetable or perennial border, allowing smaller plants to be featured in the forefront. Squashes, including pumpkins, have large, bold, sprawling leaves and usually require a lot of space along the fence or climbing up a trellis.

Fennel and bronze fennel, frilly lettuce, thyme, summer savory, oregano, curly parsley, chamomile, and dill are culinary plants with fine, lacy textures. Thai basil and globe basil must be observed up close to appreciate the intricate detail in the dainty leaves and flowers. Asparagus in late summer forms a 6 ft. (2 m) wall of wispy, fernlike foliage that creates a soft screen.

In the Watson garden, the bold, sprawling foliage of squash and cucumber surrounds blue pimpernel (*Anagallis monellii*), watercress that has gone to seed, and *Zinnia* 'Giant Enchantress' to create an interesting mix of color, foliage, and texture.

Bronze fennel produces feathery anise-flavored foliage and delicate yellow flowers that complement the lavender flowers of orange mint; both flowers attract beneficial insects to the potager.

COLOR

A potager can be filled with a variety of colors that rival any showy flower garden. Rainbow Swiss chard is one of the boldest, with its bright green, yellow, and red stalks. 'Bull's Blood' beet produces deep burgundy leaves that are both decorative and edible (in addition to the dark red edible root). Kohlrabi foliage and roots can be green, red, or purple. The cabbages and kales are green, blue-green, or pink to burgundy with touches of cream. Lettuces are available in yellows, pale greens, and various shades of red. Sage leaves can be shades of green to yellows and silvers. Basils vary from all green plants, to green plants with burgundy stems and flowers, to all red plants. Rows of purple 'Dark Opal' basil (*Ocimum basilicum* var. *purpurascens* 'Dark Opal') next to rows of dark green 'Genovese' basil provide contrasting colors that always look great in the garden.

Curly parsley's fine-textured foliage mixes well with other plants, adding rich, green texture to the garden throughout the growing season.

The heirloom 'Bull's Blood' beet is named for the color of the root vegetable growing underground as well as the edible leaves above.

Color alone can be the design directive for the garden. Consider the potager at Saint-Jean de Beauregard in France; each quadripartite bed is planted according to a different color theme that dictates the selection of the annual flowers and vegetables in the design. Try using color as the primary ordering of your design, and choose varieties of a single color when selecting seeds.

An all red (or purple-red) potager is easily achieved when you select the right varieties. A few varieties of purple basil can do the trick, such as 'Osmin', 'Red Rubin', and 'Purple Ruffles'. 'Mammoth Red Rock', purple-red cabbage, shows even coloring throughout. 'Redbor' is a hybrid kale with deep purple-red frilly leaves. 'Red Velvet' okra is a heat-loving vegetable with red stems and pods, growing 4 to 5 ft. (1.5 m) high. Huauzontle (red Aztec spinach), which grows to 4 ft. (1.5 m) in height, has red leaves that are eaten raw when young; the immature seed heads can be cooked when the plant turns bright red as it matures. Many lettuces are purple

The chartreuse leaves of *Salvia officinalis* 'Aurea' make this sage a great edger that stays compact and brightens any spot in the garden.

Perennial lavender (*Lavandula officinalis* 'Munstead') grows next to a mix of annual basils ('Genovese' and 'Cinnamon') that have been allowed to flower.

to red in color, including 'Flame', 'Lolla Rossa', 'Mascara', and 'Red Velvet'. 'Merveille des Quatre Saisons' lettuce is a French heirloom described by the seed company Vilmorin-Andrieux in *Les Plantes Potagères L'Album Vilmorin* in 1883; it is still available today.

VERTICAL FORMS

Onions, garlic, and leeks energize the potager with their striking vertical lines. This group of vegetables looks beautiful for a long period of time, adding verticality to a garden that is otherwise on one low, horizontal level. Garlic bulbs are planted in the fall; they grow underground and within weeks send up pointy shoots. Garlic leaves will fill the spring and early summer garden with deep green, spiky color, when heat-loving plants such as peppers and tomatoes are still just sprouts. Lemon grass (*Cymbopogon citrates*), a tropical plant, also produces a vertical fan of yellow-green leaves and can be tucked into beds or planted in containers.

Climbers can also be used to extend the garden vertically, to cover structures and trellises and add height to the garden. These plants impart fragrance, color, and dangling edible delights at eye level as they climb. Climbing vines become focal points in the potager, attracting attention with colorful blossoms.

The flowers and pods of runner beans are edible as well as ornamental. Hyacinth bean, with its purple ornamental pods and leaves, is a favorite

Garlic chives (*Allium tuberosum*) are easy to grow and can provide a tall perennial edge in the potager.

Onions provide a striking vertical design element in the kitchen garden.

'Heavenly Blue' morning glory (*Ipomoea tricolor* 'Heavenly Blue') is a beautiful climber; although the morning glory is not edible, it can share a trellis with edible beans or peas.

Early in the season, open the pods of a 'Scarlet Emperor' runner bean for a delightful pink surprise.

Hyacinth bean (*Dolichos lablab*) is a vigorous climber that quickly fills a pole or trellis.

CLIMBERS FOR THE POTAGER

EDIBLE

COMMON NAME	SCIENTIFIC NAME	LIFE CYCLE	COMMENTS
bitter melon	*Momordica charantia*	annual	popular in Asian cooking, can be difficult to germinate
bottle gourd	*Lagenaria siceraria*	annual	
cantaloupe	*Cucumis melo*	annual	choose small vining varieties for trellises
cucumber	*Cucumis sativus*	annual	
garden pea	*Pisum sativum*	annual	choose a climbing variety
hardy kiwi	*Actinidia arguta*	perennial, Zones 3–8	need male and female to produce small edible fruits
hops	*Humulus lupulus*	perennial, Zones 4–8	edible shoots on vigorous climber
melon 'Jenny Lind'	*Cucumis melo* var. *reticulatus* 'Jenny Lind'	annual	
green citron melon	*C. melo* var. *reticulatus* 'Vert Grimpant'	annual	
ornamental gourd	*Lagenaria* spp.	annual	
ornamental gourd	*Cucurbita* spp.	annual	
ornamental gourd	*Luffa* spp.	annual	
passion flower	*Passiflora incarnata*	perennial, Zones 6–9	edible light green fruits, can be invasive
pole bean	*Phaseolus vulgaris*	annual	
pumpkin	*Cucurbita pepo*	annual	choose small vining varieties for trellises
pumpkin 'Baby Bear'	*C. pepo* 'Baby Bear'	annual	
pumpkin 'Jack Be Little'	*C. pepo* 'Jack Be Little'	annual	
pumpkin 'Munchkin'	*C. pepo* 'Munchkin'	annual	
pumpkin 'Spooktacular'	*C. pepo* 'Spooktacular'	annual	
pumpkin 'Sweetie Pie'	*C. pepo* 'Sweetie Pie'	annual	
scarlet runner bean	*Phaseolus coccineus* 'Scarlet Emperor'	annual	edible flowers in a variety of colors

INEDIBLE

COMMON NAME	SCIENTIFIC NAME	LIFE CYCLE	COMMENTS
clematis	*Clematis* spp.	perennial, Zones 4–8	poisonous flowering vine
cross vine	*Bignonia capreolata*	perennial, Zones 6–9	flowers attract hummingbirds, U.S. native
hyacinth bean	*Dolichos lablab*	annual	vigorous climber has purple leaves, vine, flowers, and pods
morning glory	*Ipomoea purpurea*	annual	vigorous climber with poisonous flowers
sweet pea	*Lathyrus odoratus*	annual	fragrant flowers are poisonous
trumpet honeysuckle	*Lonicera sempervirens*	perennial, Zones 6–8	native species, flowers attract hummingbirds

reliable climber that quickly fills any structure and produces long-season color. As the seeds of the 'Scarlet Emperor' runner bean mature in the pods, the bright pink beans turn black with pink spots. The seeds can be eaten raw or boiled in their pods and eaten as you would edamame (the Japanese soybean). The mature seeds can also be dried for soups.

HORIZONTAL FORMS

Sprawling plants spread and overhang the edge of the bed, creating an informal mood when they blur the defining line between the raised bed and walkway. Climbing nasturtiums can be used to tumble over the edge of a raised bed or container. The purple-blossomed stems of unclipped, mature lavender can spread to soften the edge of a walkway.

Edgers are compact and tidy plants that do well in defining areas along raised beds or walkways. They range from 6 to 18 in. (15 to 46 cm) in height and are low enough to provide a border, with taller plants placed behind them. Edgers can be either annual or perennial, depending on your desire to change the look of the potager every year. A place reserved for an annual edger allows you to change from chartreuse zinnias one year to deeply savoyed (wrinkled and curled) black palm 'Nero di Toscana' kale the next year.

Espalier

Espalier is the art of training trees to grow in a flat plane along a wall or fence. This skill was perfected in the 17th century in France but was practiced earlier by the Romans in their villas and the monks in medieval monasteries. The word comes from the Italian *spallieria*, which means a shoulder (*spalla*) support. The wall provides the support for the tree and its fruit. An espaliered fruit tree can be planted along a wall when there is no room for the traditionally planted tree. Fruit trees and woody shrubs can be pruned and trained to take on a variety of shapes along a wall or fence. Espaliered fruit tree varieties are usually grafted onto dwarf root stocks to keep their final forms from growing too large; some espaliered fruit hedges can be kept at 2 ft. (61 cm) tall along a pathway or border.

Melon leaves crawl though blue pimpernel and basil, creating a dramatic sprawling leaf texture.

The orange flowers and light green foliage of *Tropaeolum majus* 'Jewel Mix' sprawl over the edges of a bed, providing an edible border plant in the potager.

EDGERS FOR THE POTAGER

COMMON NAME	SCIENTIFIC NAME	LIFE CYCLE	COMMENTS
African marigold	*Tagetes erecta*	annual	repels nematodes in soil
basil	*Ocimum basilicum*	annual	green to purple with variety of flavors
beet	*Beta vulgaris*	annual	'Bull's Blood' has red leaves
blue pimpernel	*Anagallis monellii*	perennial, Zones 7–8	highly recommended for intense blue flowers
boxwood	*Buxus* spp.	evergreen	choose small varieties and keep trimmed for a formal edge
calendula	*Calendula officinalis*	annual	yellow to orange edible flowers
catmint	*Nepeta mussinii faassenii*	perennial, Zones 3–4	choose compact varieties or keep trimmed
chive	*Allium schoenoprasum*	perennial, Zones 3–9	bright pink flowers for attractive border plant
creeping zinnia	*Zinnia angustifolia*	annual	
dianthus	*Dianthus chinensis*	annual	great for garnishes
eggplant 'Bambino'	*Solanum melongena* 'Bambino'	annual	petite variety with small purple fruits for edge
French marigold	*Tagetes patula*	annual	repels nematodes in soil
garlic chives	*Allium tuberosum*	perennial, Zone 3	
germander	*Teucrium chamaedrys*	perennial, Zones 4–9	low evergreen fragrant edger
globe amaranth	*Gomphrena globosa*	annual	
green onion	*Allium cepa*	annual	
kale	*Brassica oleracea*	annual	variety of colors, green to purple
lambs ears	*Stachys byzantina*	perennial, Zones 4–8	soft gray leaves
lavender	*Lavandula angustifolia*	perennial, Zone 5	keep trimmed for a formal edge
leek	*Allium ampeloprasum*	biennial	use as an annual
lettuce	*Lactuca sativa*	annual	variety of colors
marjoram	*Origanum marjorana*	perennial, Zones 9–10	culinary and medicinal use, keep trimmed for bushier growth
nasturtium	*Tropaeolum majus*	annual	edible flowers
ornamental pepper	*Capsicum annuum*	annual	small peppers from chartreuse to orange to red
pansy	*Viola wittrockiana*	annual	
parsley	*Petroselinum crispum*	biennial	use as an annual
rosemary	*Rosmarinus officinalis*	perennial, Zones 8–10	
sage	*Salvia officinalis*	perennial, Zones 4–10	
santolina	*Santolina chamaecyparissus*	perennial, Zones 6–9	gray-green fragrant herb
signet marigold	*Tagetes tenuifolia*	annual	aromatic
snapdragon	*Antirrhinum majus*	annual	choose dwarf varieties for edgers
sweet alyssum	*Lobularia maritima*	annual	
thyme	*Thymus vulgaris*	perennial, Zones 5–9	
viola	*Viola tricolor*	annual	edible flowers
zinnia	*Zinnia elegans*	annual	easy way to add color to the potager

'Giant of Italy' parsley is best for culinary use and can be planted close together for a long-season edger. Its dark leaves contrast well with *Calendula officinalis* 'Bon Bon Orange'.

Germander (*Teucrium chamaedrys*) provides a dainty evergreen edge in the kitchen garden.

EDIBLE WALLS

Consider adding a living, edible wall as the boundary for the potager. The wall itself will change with the seasons, flowering with fragrant blossoms in the springtime and producing colorful fruit in the summer or fall. Shrub roses vary in height, produce a long season of bloom, and produce edible hips for tea or snacking. Highbush blueberry shrubs are an attractive addition to the garden, even if the birds enjoy the fruit before you do. The shrubs grow into a thick hedge with at least three seasons of visual interest. In the fall, the leaves turn orange to red. Some varieties are evergreen year-round in climate Zones 7 to 9. Blueberries prefer acid soil, which may need to be amended, depending on your garden soil. Plant two or more varieties for pollination. Check with your county extension office for the best varieties in your zone.

Elderberries are another choice for the edible wall that looks good year-round. The shrubs are visually loose and informal, producing flowers in early summer for beverages and black fruit in the fall for jams, jellies, and wine. Some varieties grow taller than 10 ft. (3 m), but they can be kept trimmed for a more manageable hedge.

Highbush blueberry, *Vaccinium corymbosum*, from the garden at North Hill, produces sweet berries, but it also forms an attractive edible wall that provides multiseason beauty.

LIVING WALLS FOR THE POTAGER

EVERGREEN

COMMON NAME	SCIENTIFIC NAME	HEIGHT	HARDINESS ZONES	COMMENTS
American yew	*Taxus canadensis*	3–6 ft.	2	native from Canada to Midwest tolerates pruning, inedible red berries poisonous to cattle
boxwood	*Buxus* spp.	2–15 ft.	5–8	formal green hedge
glossy abelia	*Abelia* ×*grandiflora*	6–8 ft.	6–9	semi-evergreen, pinkish flowers are sometimes fragrant
holly	*Ilex crenata*	4–12 ft.	5–9	prefers acid soil
inkberry	*Ilex glabra*	4–8 ft.	5–9	

DECIDUOUS

COMMON NAME	SCIENTIFIC NAME	HEIGHT	HARDINESS ZONES	COMMENTS
alpine currant	*Ribes alpinum*	3–6 ft.	3–7	
dwarf American cranberry bush	*Viburnum trilobum* 'Compactum'	4–5 ft.	2	
gray dogwood	*Cornus recemosa*	8–12 ft.	5–8	native to eastern U.S. makes attractive informal hedge

EDIBLE

COMMON NAME	SCIENTIFIC NAME	HEIGHT	HARDINESS ZONES	COMMENTS
American black currant	*Ribes americanum*	5–6 ft.	2–6	native plant has edible black berries and prefers part shade
American elderberry	*Sambucus nigra* subsp. *canadensis*	5–12 ft.	4–9	'Adams' and 'York' varieties for fruit, tolerates shade
currant	*Ribes* spp.	4–5 ft.	3–8	some states prohibit use, choose rust-resistant varieties
flowering quince	*Chaenomeles* spp.	2–10 ft.	5–9	tart, green-yellow fruits good for jelly and flavoring, plant two varieties for fruit
highbush blueberry	*Vaccinium corymbosum*	8–10 ft.	3–7	excellent fall color, prefers acid soil, check local extension service for best varieties
raspberry	*Rubus* spp.	4–6 ft.	4–9	train on trellis, try yellow varieties
red huckleberry	*Vaccinium parvifolium*	3–5 ft.	6–9	
serviceberry	*Amelanchier alnifolia*	7–12 ft.	3–9	tolerates shade, edible fruit, multiseason color

Sunny heirloom *Calendula officinalis* (pot marigold) is easily grown from seed and is suitable for stir-fry and salad; a great addition to the potager, it was historically grown in monastery gardens.

EDIBLE FLOWERS

A walk in the potager is a pleasant way to enjoy an appetizer or a salad—pick a green bean from the vine, some lettuce, and a ripe tomato to make a fresh snack. As we nibble on plants from the garden, we realize we can put more than fresh vegetables into our salads. Growing and serving edible flowers is a natural outcome of our connection to the potager for our daily food. A wide variety of colorful edible flowers are growing in and among the vegetables. Consider adding spicy nasturtium flowers and leaves, society garlic's pungent flowers, or the slightly tangy, bitter taste of calendula to a salad.

Although many flowers may be growing in the potager, not all of them are edible, and some are actually poisonous. Morning glories contain toxins in the seeds and plants. The information on hyacinth bean is conflicting—some say the pods are poisonous when they age, and others say the pods are a Japanese delicacy. I prefer to err on the side of caution and do not eat them. All ornamental sweet peas grown for fragrance and color are poisonous and should not be confused with edible garden peas.

No flower should be eaten if it has been sprayed with pesticides or comes from a florist where it has been treated chemically. Inedible flowers have a place in the potager for use as cut flowers and to fill the garden with color and fragrance. Teach children to ask whether a flower is suitable for eating before they begin to nibble on the blossoms. Remove all inedible plants if you like, but remember that there is great joy in growing both edible and inedible flowers.

The lilac flowers of society garlic (*Tulbaghia violacea*) add a garlicky flavor to salads; they are planted here with edible bronze fennel and ornamental *Rudbeckia* 'Goldsturm'.

Nieces Kristen and Laura enjoy a tea party in the late spring garden in the midst of fragrant heirloom peonies. The table is set to enjoy strawberries, lettuce, and edible flowers from my potager.

VEGETABLES

arugula (*Eruca vesicaria* subsp. *sativa*)

garden pea (*Pisum sativum*)

scarlet runner beans (*Phaseolus coccineus*)

squash blossoms (*Cucurbita* spp.)

FLOWERS

bee balm (*Monarda didyma*)

calendula (*Calendula officinalis*)

daylily (*Hemerocallis fulva*)

dianthus (*Dianthus* spp.)

hollyhock (*Alcea rosea*)

Johnny-jump-up (*Viola tricolor*)

nasturtium (*Tropaeolum majus*)

pansy (*Viola wittrockiana*)

rose (*Rosa* spp.)

signet marigold (*Tagetes tenuifolia*)

tulip (*Tulipa* spp.)

violet (*Viola odorata*)

Edible flowers are enjoyed in the late spring garden: red nasturtiums (*Tropaeolum majus* 'Empress of India'), orange calendula (*Calendula officinalis* 'Bon Bon Orange'), lavender blossoms (*Lavandula angustifolia* 'Munstead'), purple borage flowers (*Borago officinalis*), hyssop (*Hyssopus officinalis* 'Pink Delight'), orange mint leaves (*Mentha ×piperita* f. *citrata*), and pink dianthus (*Dianthus chinensis* 'Strawberry Parfait').

Garlic chives (*Allium tuberosum*) produce edible leaves and flowers that can be used for salads, soups, and garnishes. (Photo by James E. Matson)

Tropaeolum majus 'Strawberries and Cream', like most nasturtiums, are easy to grow and edible.

DESIGN BY CUISINE

One option in laying out the planting scheme of the potager is to pair plants that belong with one another at the table. A classic pairing example is tomatoes and basil. A quick run to the garden for these two classics, especially if dinner is late, is easy—even by flashlight—if the plants are happily coexisting.

You can also design your potager according to a favorite type of recipe or by regional cooking themes. Design the garden so each square represents a culinary theme—Mexican, Asian, Mediterranean, or Italian, for example. An Italian garden would favor ingredients for traditional Italian dishes, such as paste tomatoes for sauces and drying. Study the plants' heights, widths, and cultivation requirements and consider their placement. Select each variety because of its connection to traditional Italian dishes, and include heirloom varieties from Italy.

ITALIAN CUISINE POTAGER PLANTING PLAN

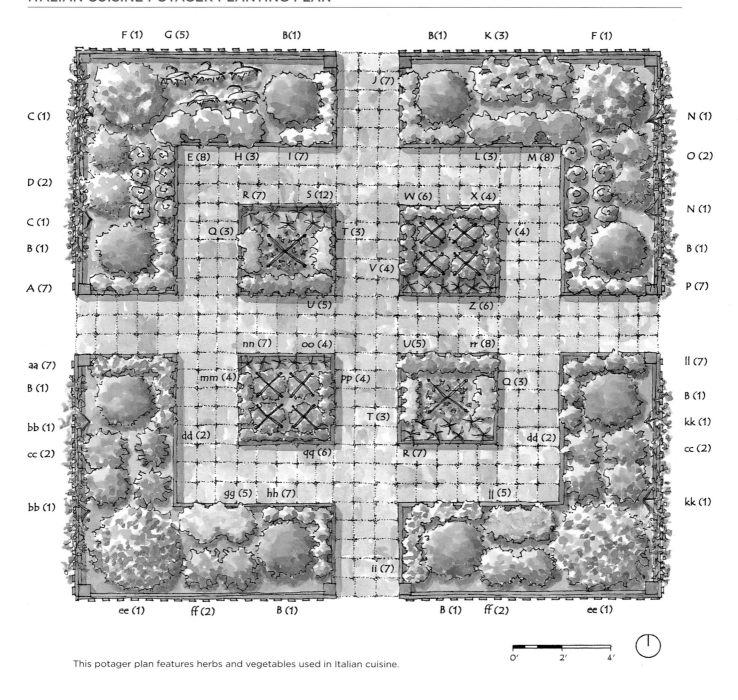

This potager plan features herbs and vegetables used in Italian cuisine.

Key

LABEL	COMMON NAME	SCIENTIFIC NAME	NO. OF PLANTS	LIFE CYCLE	COMMENTS
A	Italian oregano	*Origanum vulgare*	7	perennial, Zone 5	readily self-seeds, traditional flavoring for Italian sauces
B	boxwood	*Buxus microphylla* 'Winter Gem'	8	evergreen, Zones 4–9	evergreen shrub for year-round interest
C	sweet briar rose	*Rosa eglanteria*	2	perennial, Zones 5–9	spring-blooming pale pink heirloom rose prior to 1551, with apple-scented leaves
D	bronze fennel	*Foeniculum vulgare* 'Purpurascens'	2	perennial, Zone 6	grown for its ferny, edible, bronze leaves that attract butterflies; grows 3 ft. and self-seeds
E	escarole	*Cichorium endivia* 'Nataly'	8	annual	suitable for spring, summer, or fall planting and has mildly bitter leaves
F	'Johns' elderberry	*Sambucus canadensis* 'Johns'	2	shrub, Zones 4–9	purple-black berries are wonderful for wine or jelly
G	'Italian White' sunflower	*Helianthus cucumerifolius* 'Italian White'	5	annual	heirloom white sunflower with chocolate brown centers belongs on the shady side of the border so it will not shade other plants
H	'Prosperosa' eggplant	*Solanum melongena* 'Prosperosa'	3	annual	round heirloom variety from Tuscany
I	sweet marjoram	*Origanum marjorana*	7	perennial, Zones 9–10	grown as annual, similar to oregano but sweeter and fine textured, keep trimmed for bushy growth
J	'Lemon Gem' marigold	*Tagetes signata* 'Lemon Gem'	7	annual	light yellow edible blossoms, bushy and compact, about 1 ft. high.
K	ox eye sunflower	*Heliopsis helianthoides*	3	perennial, Zones 3–9	prairie plant attracts birds and butterflies, 3–4 ft. tall and does well at back of the border
L	eggplant	*Solanum melongena* 'Violetta Lunga'	3	annual	traditional purple Italian heirloom variety
M	radicchio	*Cichorium intybus* 'Castelfranco'	8	annual	Italian heirloom variety has cream-colored heads with specks of red
N	fennel	*Foeniculum vulgare* 'Di Firenze'	2	annual	authentic Italian variety *finocchio* produces sweet anise flavored bulbs for salads and cooking
O	'Seven Sisters' rose	*Rosa multiflora* 'Seven Sisters'	2	perennial, Zones 5–9	named for its multitude of colors, climbs 15–20 ft. and blooms once in spring and has edible hips
P	garlic chives	*Allium tuberosum*	7	perennial, Zone 3	white flowers in late August, the good edger is about 18 in. tall
Q	calendula	*Calendula officinalis* 'Radio'	6	annual	edible and easy to grow
R	'Italian Purple' garlic	*Allium sativum* 'Italian Purple'	7	annual	classic Italian hard neck variety produces large bulbs
S	'Marvel of Venice' pole bean	*Phaseolus vulgaris* 'Marvel of Venice'	16	annual	vigorous climber is an Italian heirloom with flat yellow wax beans
T	'Profusion White' zinnia	*Zinnia hybrida* 'Profusion White'	6	annual	compact white plants grow 12 in. high and bloom until frost
U	Italian parsley	*Petroselinum crispum* 'Giant of Italy'	10	biennial	dark green flat leaf variety indispensable in Italian cooking

(continued next page)

LABEL	COMMON NAME	SCIENTIFIC NAME	NO. OF PLANTS	LIFE CYCLE	COMMENTS
V	'Fino Verde' basil	*Ocimum basilicum* 'Fino Verde'	4	annual	attractive, small, flavorful leaves
W	'Genovese Compact' basil	*Ocimum basilicum* 'Genovese Compact'	6	annual	Italian pesto basil but compact in form
X	'Principe Borghese' tomato	*Solanum lycopersicum* 'Principe Borghese'	4	annual	heirloom variety excellent for sauces or drying with small, round 2 in. red fruit
Y	'Red Rubin' basil	*Ocimum basilicum* 'Red Rubin'	4	annual	purple variety with great flavor has large, striking ornamental leaves
Z	'Red Long of Tropea' shallot	*Allium cepa* 'Red Long of Tropea'	7	annual	specialty variety grown in Italy and France
aa	chives	*Allium schoenophrasum*	7	perennial, Zone 3	attractive pink flowers in early summer
bb	'White Dawn' rose	*Rosa* 'White Dawn'	2	perennial, Zones 5–9	repeat blooming white rose dating to 1949 is very fragrant and climbs 12 to 20 ft.
cc	cannellini bean	*Phaseolus vulgaris* 'Cannellini'	4	annual	white kidney shell bean on large plants can be dried and used for minestrone soup
dd	bull's horn pepper	*Capsicum annuum* 'Corno di Toro Rosso'	4	annual	mild Italian pepper turns bright red
ee	red currant	*Ribes rubrum* 'Jhonkheer Van Tets'	2	shrub, Zones 3–8	red fruit clusters in early summer on a mildew- and aphid-resistant shrub, 4–5 ft. tall
ff	'Borlotti' bean	*Phaseolus vulgaris* 'Borlotti'	4	annual	Italian heirloom variety grows like bush beans, with pink and maroon beans used in soups and stews
gg	'Cosmic Yellow' cosmos	*Cosmos sulphureus* 'Cosmic Yellow'	5	annual	compact yellow flowers require no deadheading
hh	rosemary	*Rosmarinus officinalis*	7	perennial, Zones 8–10	use in foccacia, treated as an annual where not hardy
ii	thyme	*Thymus vulgaris*	7	perennial, Zones 5–9	compact herb produces purple to pink flowers in summer
jj	'Peach Melba' nasturtium	*Tropaeolum majus nanum* 'Peach Melba Superior Wina'	5	annual	pale yellow with dark blue-green foliage
kk	'Marchioness of Londonderry' rose	*Rosa* 'Marchioness of Londonderry'	2	perennial, Zones 5–9	repeat bloomer dates from 1893 and climbs 5–8 ft., with large pink blooms
ll	rue	*Ruta graveolens*	7	perennial, Zones 4–9	blue-green herb grows to about 18 in.
mm	'Magical Michael' basil	*Ocimum basilicum* 'Magical Michael'	4	annual	compact variety grows 10–14 in. with long-lasting red flowers
nn	'Deep Purple' bunching onion	*Allium* 'Deep Purple'	8	annual	sow in spring for summer use and fall for overwintering, deep red-purple stays true at any temperature
oo	'Purple Ruffles' basil	*Ocimum basilicum* 'Purple Ruffles'	4	annual	large ruffled purple leaves and pink flowers
pp	'Cuor di Bue' tomato	*Solanum lycopersicum* 'Cuor di Bue'	4	annual	large Italian heirloom tomato with oxheart shape
qq	'Napoletano' basil	*Ocimum basilicum* 'Napoletano'	6	annual	large frilly leaves lighter in color than other pesto basils
rr	'Zucchino Rampicante' squash	*Cucurbita moschata* 'Zucchino Rampicante'	8	annual	grown on a trellis, Italian heirloom vining zucchini is long and thin with a flat bulb at the bottom; harvest when small

CROP ROTATION

The garden plan should incorporate the art of *crop rotation*—the practice of rotating plants from the same botanical plant family on a yearly basis. For example, plants from the Solanaceae, or nightshade family, should not be planted in the same spot every year. Peppers, tomatoes, potatoes, and eggplant are all in this family, which means you shouldn't plant a tomato where potatoes were grown the previous year, for example. Plant families share the same foliar diseases and insects, which can remain in the soil even after the plants are removed. Fusarium wilt in tomatoes is an example of a fungus that lives in the soil for years. It enters the plant through the roots, destroying the vascular tissue and killing the plant.

The goal of crop rotation, then, is to prevent disease in the garden, and the extra effort you spend in planning may prevent crop loss from diseases. In the small garden, crop rotation is more difficult if plants are intermixed, but planting in rows and blocks of space eases the rotation schedule. Allow a rotation schedule of at least three years. Create and keep detailed planting plans every year to aid your memory when seed catalogs arrive and next year's dreaming begins.

A four-year crop rotation schedule works well for the quadripartite garden. In the simplest system, crops are planted in a different bed each year. Blocks of families are rotated within the beds and then into the other beds.

The drawings on the following pages show a four-year crop rotation plan for my small residential potager, which is discussed further in Chapter 7. (The year 1 planting plan, not shown here, is shown in Chapter 7.) I have used colors and letters to represent each of the botanical families grown in my garden. Not every plant family is included; this is a small garden and I plant only my favorite vegetables. I do not plant okra from the mallow family (Malvaceae) every year, but I do put in peppers, tomatoes, and parsley annually. I have included basil from the mint family because it is planted every year and is therefore part of the rotation schedule.

CROP ROTATION PLAN

Crop rotation plan year 2

Crop rotation plan year 3

Crop rotation plan year 4

Key

This chart shows the botanical plant families and many common vegetables included in each rotation in my garden, as indicated by labels in the drawings. The general and simple rule to follow is this: never plant from the same family in the same space in successive years. This is an ideal goal and most appropriate for the larger scale organic farmer, but it is worth attempting in the small garden as well.

LABEL	FAMILY	PLANTS
A	Apiaceae, carrot family	carrot, celeriac, celery, chervil, coriander, dill, fennel, parsnip, parsley
B	Asteraceae, sunflower family	calendula, endive, Jerusalem artichoke, lettuce, salsify
C	Brassicaceae, mustard family	bok choy, broccoli, brussels sprouts, cabbage, cauliflower, Chinese cabbage, collards, cress, horseradish, kale, kohlrabi, mustard greens, radish, rutabaga, turnip
D	Chenopodiaceae, goosefoot family	beet, spinach, Swiss chard
E	Cucurbitaceae, gourd family	cucumber, gourd, muskmelon, pumpkin, squash, watermelon
F	Fabaceae, pea family	lima bean, pea, snap bean, soybean
G	Lamiaceae, mint family	basil
H	Malvaceae, mallow family	okra
I	Solanaceae, nightshade family	eggplant, pepper, potato, tomato
L	Lamiaceae	lavender, a perennial, not rotated

'Bambino' eggplant, santolina (*Santolina chamaecyparissus*), and hyacinth bean grow side by side in my potager.

MIXING PERENNIALS AND VEGETABLES

I used to have a romantic notion about planting perennials with the vegetables or tucking vegetables in among the flowers, and for years I planted peppers and basil next to the perennial daisies and okra, and tomatoes in among the rue and chamomile. However, I found it difficult to prepare the soil yearly, lest I disturb the roots of the existing perennial plants. To resolve this dilemma, I removed all the perennials except the lavender edgers from my main vegetable beds so I had the freedom to dig in the soil and mix in compost.

Ancient wisdom in the medieval monastic tradition suggests planting the medicinal garden separately from the vegetable garden. The medicinal garden, or garden of simples, was planted with a variety of herbs and perennials used for healing. This bed would lie undisturbed during seasonal chores in the vegetable plots. Allowing the perennial and annual plants their own space is more convenient and simplifies maintenance.

Perennials and shrubs can be used to form edges and borders to the potager, however, and they can be planted just outside the fence or wall. Perennial vegetables, such as rhubarb and asparagus, can be planted with perennial flowers tucked in around the edges or outside the vegetable garden. Annual flowers can easily be added to the vegetable plot and make good partners with annual vegetables.

Marigold 'Snowball Hybrid' is planted as an edging next to tomatoes.

Companion planting

My friend Holly called just to thank me for encouraging her to add marigolds, zinnias, and nasturtiums to her kitchen garden. She said, "Every morning before work, I have my coffee in the garden. It is such a joy."

Not only do flowers look beautiful in the vegetable garden, but they serve a constructive purpose. The colorful blossoms are working hard to attract beneficial insects and birds to the garden. These flowers provide nectar and pollen to nourish the predatory insects that feed on other insects that are munching holes in your beans, eggplant, and kale. These friendly insects with names like big-eyed bug, minute pirate bug, assassin bug, and soldier beetle prey on the larvae of destructive beetles and moths, aphids, and other insects.

Coneflowers and sunflowers, with their tasty seeds, attract a variety of birds to the garden, and bright flowers attract hummingbirds. The birds will feed on insects as well. Tucking these flowers in among your vegetables or just outside the potager fence or wall will help you achieve a balance in the garden by attracting a variety of wildlife. This is a simplified version of companion planting that doesn't require a grand, complex plan. Just mix up the annual cutting flowers from the accompanying list with your vegetables.

Daylilies (*Hemerocallis*) and anise hyssop (*Agastache foeniculum*) are edible and do well as cut flowers. They also add diversity and attract beneficial insects to the potager.

Plants that nourish beneficial insects

COMMON NAME	SCIENTIFIC NAME	LIFE CYCLE
angelica, alexanders	*Angelica* spp.	perennial
anise hyssop	*Agastache foeniculum*	perennial
aster	*Aster alpinus, A. tataricus*	perennial
bachelor's buttons	*Centaurea cyanus*	annual
basil	*Ocimum basilicum*	annual
basket of gold	*Aurinia saxatilis*	perennial
bee balm	*Phacelia tanacetifolia*	annual
birds eyes	*Gilia tricolor*	annual
bishop's weed	*Ammi majus*	perennial
blanketflower	*Gaillardia* spp.	perennial
blue cardinal flower	*Lobelia siphilitica*	perennial
blue lace flower	*Trachymene coerulea*	annual
borage	*Borago officinalis*	annual
calendula	*Calendula officinalis*	annual
California poppy	*Eschscholzia californica*	annual
candytuft	*Iberis umbellata*	annual
catmint	*Nepeta*	perennial
chervil	*Anthriscus cerefolium*	annual
cinquefoil	*Potentilla*	perennial
comfrey	*Symphytum*	perennial
coneflower	*Echinacea*	perennial

COMMON NAME	SCIENTIFIC NAME	LIFE CYCLE
coral vine	*Antigonon leptopus*	perennial
coreopsis	*Coreopsis*	perennial
coriander	*Coriandrum sativum*	annual
corn	*Zea mays*	annual
corn poppy	*Papaver rhoeas*	annual
cosmos	*Cosmos bipinnatus*	annual
cup plant	*Silphium perfoliatum*	perennial
dill	*Anethum graveolens*	annual
evening primrose	*Oenothera biennis*	perennial
fennel	*Foeniculum vulgare*	perennial
feverfew	*Chrysanthemum parthenium*	perennial
garlic chives	*Allium tuberosum*	perennial
golden marguerite	*Anthemis tinctoria*	perennial
goldenrod	*Solidago*	perennial
green lace flower	*Ammi visnaga*	perennial
Jerusalem artichoke	*Helianthus tuberosus*	perennial
Korean mint	*Agastache rugosa*	perennial
lavender	*Lavandula angustifolia*	perennial
lobelia	*Lobelia erinus*	annual
lovage	*Levisticum officinale*	perennial
lupine	*Lupinus*	perennial
meadow foam	*Limnanthes douglasii*	annual
Mexican sunflower	*Tithonia rotundifolia*	annual
milkweed	*Asclepias*	perennial
mint	*Mentha*	perennial
mountain mint	*Pycnanthemum muticum, P. virginianum*	perennial
mountain sandwort	*Arenaria montana*	perennial
peony	*Paeonia*	perennial
pincushion flower	*Scabiosa atropurpurea*	annual
pincushion flower	*Scabiosa caucasica*	perennial
poppy mallow	*Callirhoe involucrata*	perennial
Rocky Mountain penstemon	*Penstemon strictus*	perennial
sea lavender	*Limonium latifolium*	perennial
sea pink	*Armeria alliacea*	perennial
sedum	*Sedum album, S. kamtschaticum, S. spurium*	perennial
signet marigold	*Tagetes signata*	annual
sunflower	*Helianthus annuus*	annual
sweet alyssum	*Lobularia maritima*	annual
sweet marjoram	*Origanum majorana*	annual
tansy	*Tanacetum vulgare* var. *crispum*	perennial
teasel	*Dipsacus*	perennial
thrift	*Armeria maritima*	perennial
tidy tips	*Layia platyglossa*	annual
wild bergamot	*Monarda fistulosa*	perennial
wood betony	*Stachys officinalis*	perennial
yarrow	*Achillea*	perennial

Adapted from Cheryl Long, "Beneficial Borders," on the *Organic Gardening* magazine website, http://www. organicgardening.com/ (accessed August 2005)

Yellow-flowering purple kale and lacy fennel grow well in containers when potager space is limited.

CHAPTER SEVEN

Potager Designs

THIS CHAPTER PROVIDES EXAMPLES of potager designs for a variety of settings. I created two restaurant potagers for chefs in urban settings, and I created my own suburban potager. Also included are some small garden sketches appropriate for specific situations—an edible garden for full shade conditions and a low-maintenance edible perennial garden, in which a small vignette of movable pots was added to demonstrate that the potager philosophy does not have to be grand but begins with a useful herb, flower, or vegetable—even one planted in a simple clay pot.

BLUE STEEL GARDEN
An ideal urban potager

I designed the Blue Steel garden in Columbus, Ohio, to illustrate the potential of reusing empty spaces in urban areas and transforming an underutilized enclosed area into a fruitful garden. The design demonstrates how existing buildings can be used as walls and edges for a potager and shows that kitchen gardens can be planted where they are most needed—even next to urban restaurants. I analyzed the existing conditions of the site, explored a variety of design options, and then created a design with an extensive plant list. Although the garden was not actually built, the lessons I learned while designing this space can be applied to any gardening situation, urban or suburban.

The space between an office building and a restaurant in Columbus, Ohio, is an ideal location for an urban potager that would be an oasis in the midst of the city. (Photo by Franklin County GIS)

The site

The site is in the center of a network of highways and abandoned warehouses being refurbished and converted to office spaces and lofts. The garden space is formed primarily by two historical buildings. The first wall is the side of a six-story building that was renovated and converted to offices that overlook the open space selected for the potager. The eastern edge of the space is formed by a two-story restaurant with overlooking windows. The area between these two brick buildings is an unused swath of lawn, ideal for an herb, flower, fruit, and vegetable garden. This garden could serve

The view of the existing space, facing the arborvitae to the north; the current lawn space has potential as an urban potager.

the restaurant with seasonal flowers and produce while providing a visual feast for the patrons as they dine at tables overlooking the potager.

An existing row of evergreen arborvitae creates a sense of enclosure on the north side of the lawn and separates the space from the rear parking lot. These trees are in fair condition, but the edge of the space could be strengthened with additional plant material to shield the garden visually from the parking lot. A gate is located in the center of the row of evergreens and provides an entrance from the parking lot to the rear of the buildings.

A concrete sidewalk surrounds the existing central green space and abuts each building. This sidewalk could remain in place to provide access around the potager, but the paving material should complement the design of the garden. The south end of the garden is open and provides a view of the downtown area. In addition, a blue steel structure provides a sense of enclosure while allowing light to enter the garden. The steel structure is a very important feature of this urban site; it clearly defines the space yet leaves it open, so people can see into and out of the garden, allowing for enclosure but not a feeling of entrapment. The blue steel theme could be repeated in additional garden structures to add a sense of continuity to the overall design.

The restaurant windows overlook the space, but the garden cannot be accessed from these floor-to-ceiling first-floor windows. The six-story building has large windows on the west side overlooking the garden, so workers in the offices within the building can gaze down upon the garden. The blue metal framework of the windows forms a grid pattern, and the strong geometric forms should be reflected in the garden to unify its design with the existing building.

The existing blue steel structure provides a sense of enclosure without being confining in this public urban space.

The plan view of the site shows the relationship of the existing buildings to the kitchen garden.

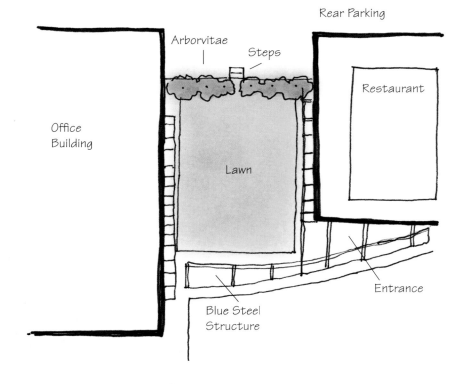

An urban *hortus conclusus* is formed by two buildings and a row of existing arborvitae; the enclosure is completed by the existing blue steel structure.

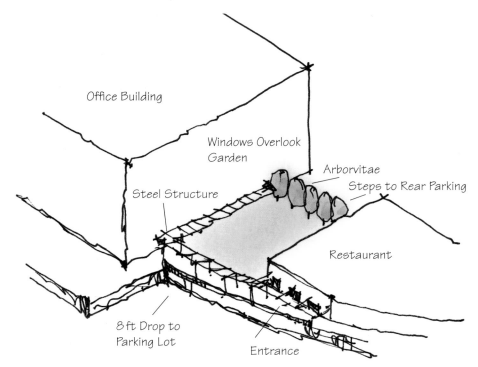

Technical studies and site analysis

I conducted shadow studies using charts appropriate for local latitude and measuring the shadow distance based on the angle of the sun and heights of the buildings. (Another way to measure shadow is to observe the site at different times during the growing season, but such observation isn't

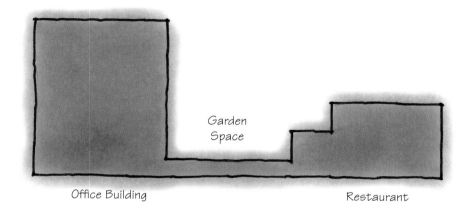

Garden Space

Office Building   Restaurant

In the view looking north, the figure-ground spatial study shows the heights of the buildings relative to one another, revealing the volume of the space.

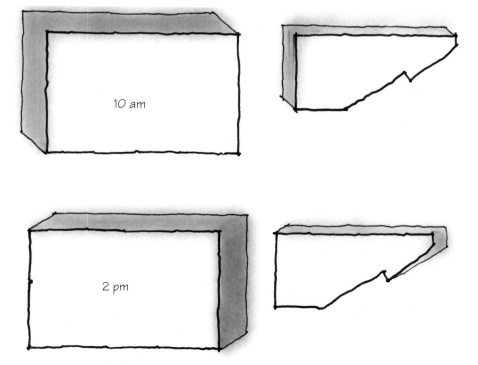

10 am

2 pm

The shadow study shows the length of the buildings' shadows during the month of June, at 10 a.m. and 2 p.m. The western half of the site will receive only morning sunlight.

always possible.) The studies revealed that the entire site does not receive a full six hours of sunlight in June. Half the area receives only four hours of morning sunlight, but this is sufficient for some leafy vegetables and flowers that require part-sun conditions. This presents a design opportunity to brighten up the shady space with colorful edible or cutting flowers of white, yellow, and orange. This part-sun spot will extend the growing time of cool-season vegetables that would wilt in the heat of the summer sun.

The grid structure of the windows is an important facet of the design, but a new grid can be used for the garden that responds to but is not rigidly constrained by the structure of the windows. I designed the site using a 3 ft. (1 m) grid, which became a gauge for the layout of the raised beds and walkways. A 3 ft. (1 m) walkway through the garden would allow for ease of strolling along the path and ample room for a wheelchair or a wheelbarrow or cart for maintenance. Doubling this dimension to 6 ft. (2 m) is an ideal length and width for the raised beds, allowing the plants to be reached from any side.

In short, site analysis and study suggested that we should

* Strengthen the northern edge of the garden (arborvitae area).

* Use the color blue in the garden because it was already used predominately in the site. Other colors should be introduced to complement/counterpoint the blue.

* Reflect the grid pattern used in the metal windows in the garden.

* Select appropriate edible plants that tolerate some shade, because the western half of the site will receive only four hours of sun in June.

Contrasting colors will provide visual interest.

Vertical poles can be used for climbing vines.

Conceptual studies

I developed concept sketches for the site, showing color, texture, and height relationships. Lacy green lettuce placed next to red cabbage would produce a pleasing contrast. Poles or other structures would add vertical elements on which runner beans or other vines could climb.

Design concept sketches are helpful in trying out a variety of forms to see which is the most pleasing. This process is fun and involves asking questions and testing the answers. In this case, I asked and tested the following questions: "What happens if I use the grid but turn it on its side? What if I slant the grid so it is not running parallel and perpendicular to the buildings? How would a counterpoint design using rigid, rectilinear planting boxes with an overlay of curvilinear planting look?" Ultimately, I selected a maze concept for further development because of its formal plan view, reflection of the strong grid structure of the building windows, and evocation of kitchen garden forms in French potagers.

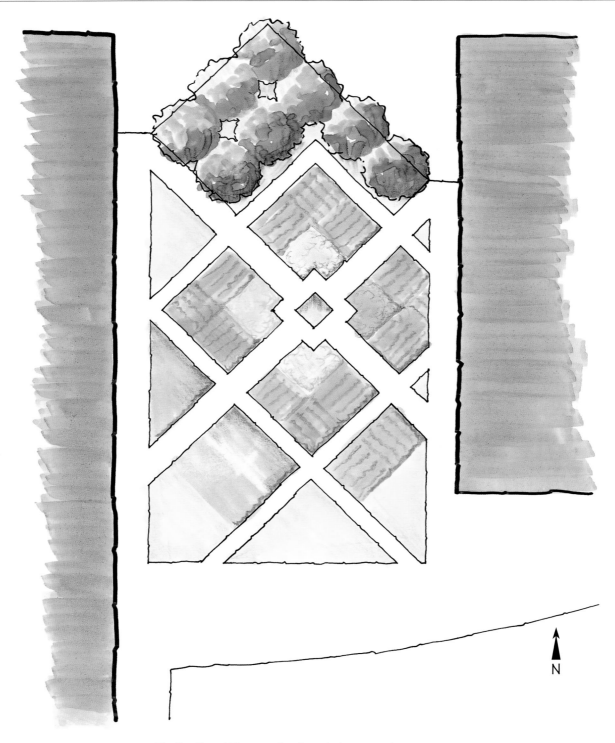

Slanting the grid is one option for a design concept.

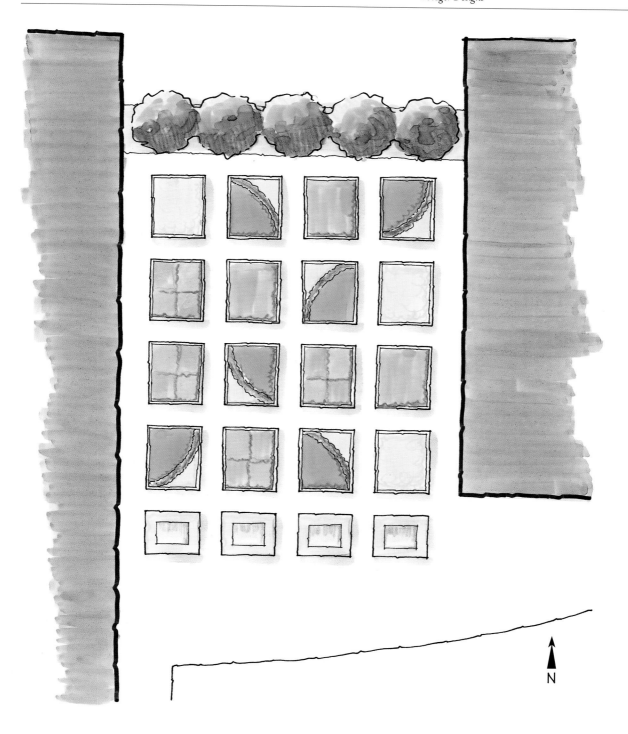

The curvilinear planting provides interesting contrast in the grid layout.

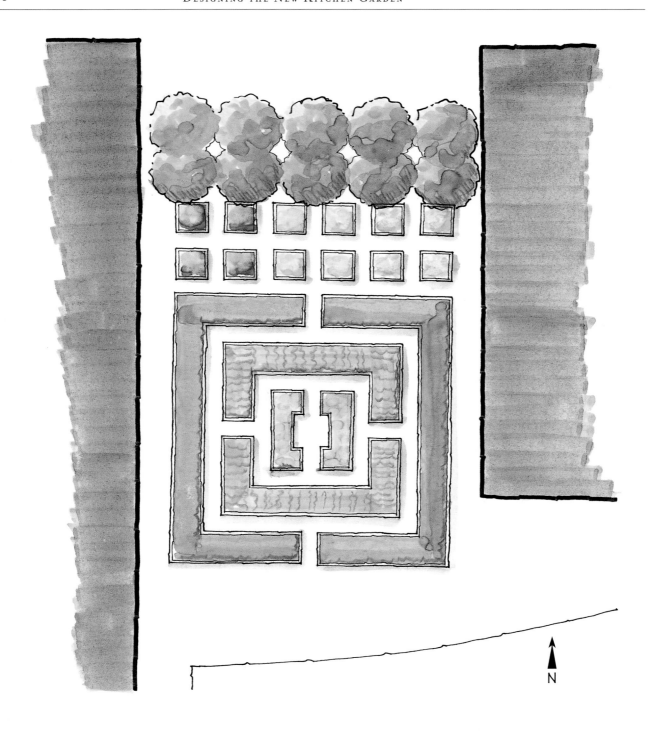

The maze garden layout was best because of its formal plan view, reflection of the windows' grid structure, and evocation of French potager forms.

FINAL ILLUSTRATIVE DESIGN

I designed the potager using a ¼ in. architect's scale (¼ in. = 1 ft.), so the specific plants and details of the garden could easily be seen. All of the herbs, flowers, vegetables, and fruit trees are either edible or have historical medicinal purposes. The layout of the gardens is symmetrical, which is appropriate for this central plaza space. No single door allows entrance into the garden; instead, each direction has its own entrance.

Humulus lupulus is used to make beer, and the shoots are edible.

The final garden plan consists of four areas named Shade 1, Shade 2, Sun 1, and Sun 2, reflecting sun requirements for each area. The planting plan is not symmetrical, so the experience as the visitor travels through the garden would be different in each area. Each of the four quadrants has a color theme. Shade 1 and Sun 2 have primarily yellow, green, and white vegetables, herbs, and flowers. Shade 2 and Sun 1 contain primarily herbs and vegetables with blue, purple, or red colors in the leaves, stems, or flowers.

The herb garden consists of a dozen 6-by-6-ft. (2-by-2 m) square raised beds. The beds are 12 in. (31 cm) high and built of untreated cedar. Each of the beds is edged with boxwood to provide uniformity to the design and year-round structure and color. Each bed features a different planting, and each bed contains only one other type of plant in addition to the boxwood. Included in these plantings are rosemary, bronze fennel, dill, chervil, cilantro, French sorrel, tarragon, hyssop, lavender, sage, yellow mustard, and lemon balm.

The center of the garden is defined by four metal pergolas, each 8 ft. (2.5 m) tall and painted to match the bed scheme. *Humulus lupulus* (hops), a vigorous climbing vine that grows 12 to 15 ft. (3.5 to 4.5 m), will cover the blue and purple pergolas. The hops are fragrant and can be used to make beer; shoots of the plant are also edible, with a flavor reminiscent of asparagus. The yellow and orange pergolas are planted with runner beans: 'Scarlet Runner', an heirloom variety grown in 18th century America, climbs to 18 ft. (5.5 m) and produces red flowers in addition to edible beans. 'Painted Lady' produces red and white bicolored flowers.

I added six Mirabelle plum trees (*Prunus insititia* 'Mirabelle de Nancy') to the design of the lower level near the parking lot to provide additional screening. The scented blossoms would create a pleasant experience in the spring, and the trees produce small fruits with yellow flesh and red dots on the skin that ripen in August. The plums are sweet and excellent for tarts, jams, and snacking. The existing arborvitae will remain in the final design for a year-round screen.

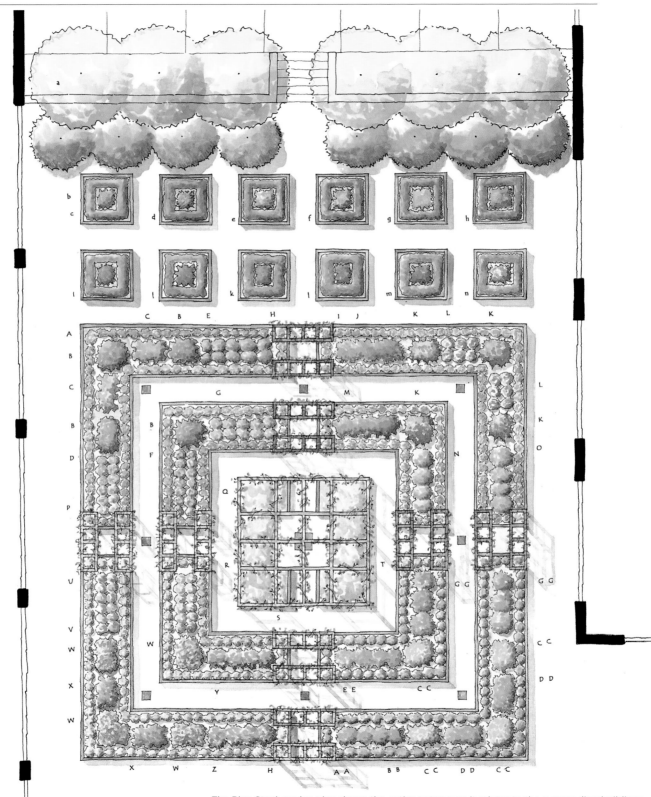

The Blue Steel garden plan shows the entire potager as it relates to the surrounding buildings.

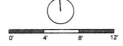

0'   4'   8'   12'

Key

LABEL	COMMON NAME	SCIENTIFIC NAME	COMMENTS
a	plum	*Prunus insititia* 'Mirabelle de Nancy'	small, sweet yellow fruits
b	boxwood	*Buxus*	evergreen edge for year-round color
c	yellow mustard	*Sinapis alba* subsp. *alba*	
d	rosemary	*Rosmarinus officinalis*	treat as an annual in Zone 5
e	hyssop	*Hyssopus officinalis*	
f	lavender	*Lavandula angustfolia*	fragrant flowers
g	lemon balm	*Melissa officinalis* 'Aurea'	
h	bronze fennel	*Foeniculum vulgare* 'Purpurascens'	feathery bronze leaves are good in salads
i	chervil	*Anthriscus cerefolium*	mild herb for cooking
j	French sorrel	*Rumex scutatus*	traditionally used in soup
k	cilantro	*Coriandrum sativum*	pungent herb for Mexican cooking
l	dill	*Anethum graveolens*	readily self-seeds
m	French tarragon	*Artemisia dracunculus*	
n	sage	*Salvia officinalis*	
A	'Creamsicle' nasturtium	*Tropaeolum majus* 'Creamsicle'	sherbet-orange edible flowers
B	black cohosh	*Cimicifuga racemosa*	endangered species in the wild
C	'Victoria' rhubarb	*Rheum rhabarbarum* 'Victoria'	recommended for Midwest gardens
D	lettuce	*Lactuca sativa* 'Matchless'	dates in the U.S. to the 1740s
E	pak choi	*Brassica rapa* 'Joi Choi'	
F	lettuce	*Lactuca sativa* 'Paris White Cos'	originated in France before 1868
G	sprouting broccoli	*Brassica oleracea* 'De Cicco'	small, Italian variety of sprouting broccoli
H	hops	*Humulus lupulus*	fragrant vine 12–15 ft. with edible shoots
I	chives	*Allium schoenoprasum*	edible stems and pink edible flowers
J	asparagus	*Asparagus officinalis*	perennial
K	lavender	*Lavandula angustifolia*	
L	red cabbage	*Brassica oleracea* 'Mammoth Red Rock'	
M	globe artichoke	*Cynara* (Scolymus Group) 'Green Globe'	
N	eggplant	*Solanum melongena* 'Listada de Gandia'	Italian variety
O	eggplant	*S. melongena* 'Rosa Bianca'	Italian variety
P	scarlet runner bean	*Phaseolus coccineus* 'Scarlet Emperor'	in America before 1750
Q	apple	*Malus*	shaped as a cordon here
R	white cosmos	*Cosmos bipinnatus* 'Versailles White'	reaches height of 4–6 ft.
S	cleome	*Cleome hasslerana*	self-seeding
T	runner bean	*Phaseolus coccineus* 'Painted Lady'	in America since 1827, bicolored flowers
U	thyme	*Thymus vulgaris*	
V	leaf lettuce	*Lactuca sativa* 'Red Sails'	
W	borage	*Borago officinalis*	edible blue flowers attract pollinating bees
X	celery	*Apium graveolens* var. *dulce* 'Red Stalk'	dark red stalks remain red even after cooking
Y	purple basil	*Ocimum basilicum* 'Red Rubin	purple version of Italian large leaf basil
Z	sweet Thai basil	*Ocimum basilicum* 'Sweet Thai'	purple stems and blossoms, most used basil in Thailand
AA	Italian parsley	*Petroselinum crispum*	flat, glossy dark green leaves best for cooking
BB	'Italian Large Leaf' basil	*Ocimum basilicum* 'Italian Large Leaf'	height to 20–24 in.
CC	Jerusalem artichoke	*Helianthus tuberosus* 'Stampede'	perennial sunflower grown for its potatolike tubers and chocolate-scented flowers
DD	fennel	*Foeniculum vulgare* 'Zefa Fino'	above-ground bulb has an anise flavor
EE	lemon basil	*Ocimum basilicum citriodora* 'Mrs. Burns' Lemon'	heirloom variety with white flower bracts has strong lemon scent
GG	heirloom tomato	*Solanum lycopersicum* 'Green Grape', 'Green Zebra', 'Persimmon', 'San Marzano', 'White Wonder'	

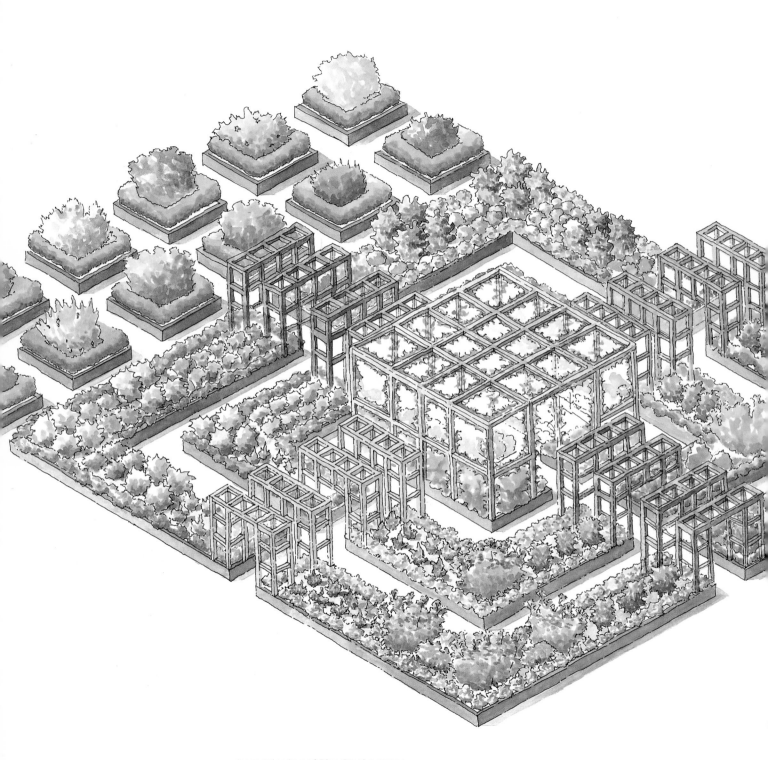

Isometric view of Blue Steel potager.

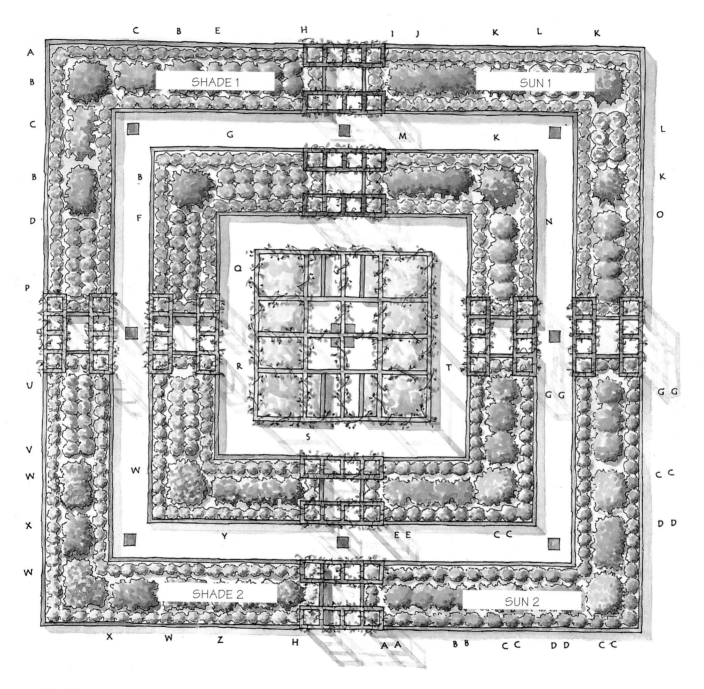

The Blue Steel potager planting plan, with the designated areas of the potager shown: Shade 1, Shade 2, Sun 1, and Sun 2.

A section showing the secret
garden in the center of the potager.

Secret garden

In the center of the garden, another metal structure forms a "secret" garden
with a small fountain, 2 by 2 ft. (60 by 60 cm) square. The fountain serves
as a surprise feature for visitors who enter the secret garden. Four small
jets swell up like rose blossoms, and pale-colored lights would add to this
illusion at night. A variety of apple trees would be pruned in cordons to
cover the structure. The trees would eventually cover the metal structure
and form a perfect grid of fruit covering the trained branches. White
cosmos and self-seeding cleome would be planted in the central raised
beds. These annual flowers would provide a light and airy opaque screen of
3 to 4 ft. (1 m) high.

Shade 1

The colors orange, white, and green predominate in this corner of the
garden. 'Creamsicle' nasturtiums are featured along the edges of the raised
beds. This variety produces edible, sherbet-orange flowers mounding over
green foliage. 'Victoria' rhubarb, a perennial with large bold leaves and
sweet green stalks, is included in the planting next to black cohosh, which
produces white lacy spikes of flowers. Pak choi, 'Paris White Cos' lettuce,
and Italian sprouting broccoli are included. 'Deer Tongue' lettuce, an
heirloom variety, produces green rosettes.

Shade 2

In this area, each plant was selected for its purple or red coloring on foliage, stems, or flowers. 'Red Sails' leaf lettuce has red, curly leaves; planting seed every few weeks ensures a continual supply of the lettuce. Borage, with edible blue-purple flowers, appears at the four corners—the outside corners of the area. 'Red Stalk' celery stalks retain their intense red color even after cooking. Sweet Thai basil, the most commonly used basil in Thailand, produces purple stems and blossoms. 'Red Rubin' is another purple variety basil. Thyme surrounds the edges with its pinkish purple flowers.

A chef picks nasturtiums for a salad.

Sun 1

This area of the garden features chive borders, which produce bright pink-purple flowers. The four corners area is dominated by lavender, with its fragrant edible flowers. 'Mammoth Red Rock' is a decorative red cabbage. Two kinds of Italian purple eggplant are used: 'Listada de Gandia' and 'Rosa Bianca'. Asparagus is a perennial with light green, airy foliage to 4 ft. (1 m) in addition to purplish asparagus shoots in the early spring. Globe artichoke, with its bold textured leaves, is a perennial, but it must be grown as an annual in this climate.

Sun 2

Yellow and green are the colors that predominate in this area of the garden. At the four corners near a small blue tile in the walkway is Jerusalem artichoke, a perennial sunflower grown for its potatolike tubers. It grows 6 to 8 ft. (2 to 2.5 m) tall and produces 4 in. (10 cm) flowers with the scent of chocolate. Placed between the sunflowers is 'Zefa Fino' fennel, with very delicate foliage and an above-ground bulb with an anise flavor. 'Mrs. Burns' Lemon' basil, a lemon-scented heirloom variety, is placed near the heirloom tomatoes 'Green Zebra' and 'White Wonder'. 'Italian Large Leaf' basil is also planted here. The beds are surrounded with the biennial Italian parsley, the flat leaf variety that is best for cooking.

DRAGONFLY NEO-V CUISINE
A chef's garden in the city

I was pleased to consult with Magdiale Wolmark of Dragonfly Neo-V Cuisine in Columbus, Ohio, during some of the early creation stages of his kitchen garden. As in all garden design, the constraints and opportunities of the site and the needs of the client influenced my conceptual design of this garden. Magdiale intends to have the garden certified by the Ohio Ecological Food and Farm Association; therefore, all of the seeds in the design should come from certified organic sources—these are available from many seed companies. Magdiale hopes to grow unique vegetable varieties that are not readily available from his growers and microgreens that are too fragile to transport. His vision is to inspire others with what can be grown in an urban garden and to educate neighborhood children about growing food.

The garden site

The three-story brick building that houses the restaurant faces north, and although Magdiale has outdoor restaurant seating here, this is no place to grow flowers and vegetables. The rear of the restaurant faces south and receives ample summer light for vegetable growing. The problem is space; this tiny area is covered in blacktop dominated by a large trash enclosure.

Site of Dragonfly Neo-V Cuisine site (Photo by Franklin County GIS)

However, moving the trash area to another location and removing the enclosure will create room for a sunny garden. The south-facing red brick walls are ideal for espaliered fruit trees placed flat against the warm walls. Vertical space can be used throughout this garden. Eventually, a grid of containers can be planted up the wall and onto the sunny roof, as Magdiale dreams of a rooftop greenhouse.

The rear garden space is surrounded by open parking lots to the east and south. No buildings block the southern sun, but the space is not framed and provides no privacy and enclosure; the space simply opens to the parking lots. Planting trees or shrubs along this property line is not feasible because of lack of space. However, a fence could be erected to hold climbing vines.

Removal of the trash receptacle and blacktop creates a space at the rear of the building large enough for a garden with enough sun to grow vegetables.

The restaurant needs an open pathway to the kitchen door for deliveries of organic vegetables and sulfite-free wine. A paved walkway must remain open from the alley to the kitchen door so that delivery carts can be rolled to the kitchen unobstructed.

My site analysis and study revealed these recommendations:

* Remove unused trash enclosure.

* Provide space for a service area and make use of movable trash bins.

* Create a fence for enclosure and privacy and provide space for climbing beans, peas, and flowers. The fence should be 6 ft. (2 m) high but should be of an open design to allow light to penetrate the site.

* Keep the path to the kitchen door accessible from the alley to allow deliveries to the kitchen.

* Replace asphalt with brick pathways.

* Create 1 ½ ft. (46 cm) raised beds to ensure an adequate depth for vegetables, flowers, and small shrubs; import soil to the site.

* Create overhead structures that will serve as sculptural elements as well as trellises for climbing vines.

These concept renderings focused on creating a green oasis in the city.

Conceptual design

I developed conceptual photographs to show my vision of the garden—an urban, green paradise. Although all my ideas didn't make it into the final design, they did contribute to it.

Eventually, I drew up two design concepts and showed them to Magdiale. The first concept featured "rollaway beds"—a series of metal boxes on wheels that could be moved at different times of the year for special events or stored when not in use. I created an isometric sketch to visualize the space.

The second concept used long beds consisting of permanent, linear raised beds with walkways. This concept left room for an outdoor eating cove. Magdiale preferred this scenario, because it made the best use of precious space and preserved an area for the chef's table near the kitchen door.

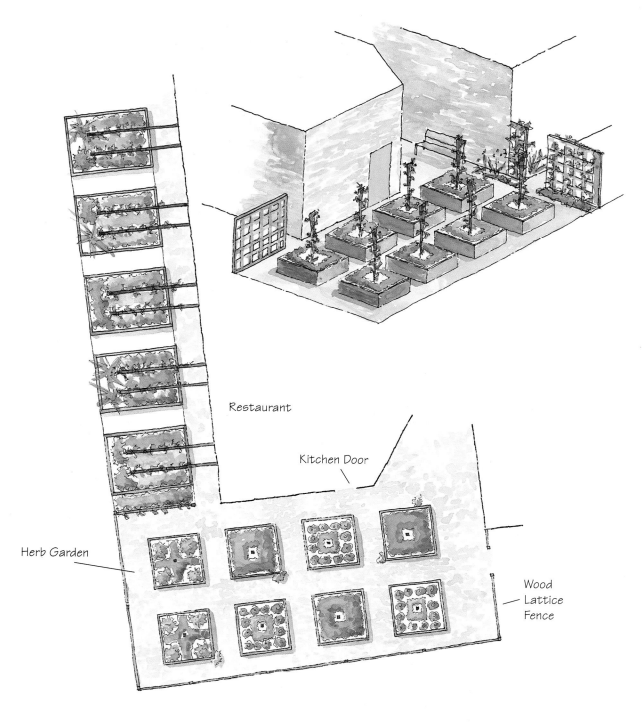

Restaurant

Kitchen Door

Herb Garden

Wood
Lattice
Fence

The "rollaway beds" concept shows part of the wood lattice fence that would surround the garden to create an intimate potager.

I drew up this design with a scale of 1 in. = 4 ft. In the plan, the raised planting beds and the outline of the fence enclosure are shown. Access to the kitchen door is from the alley for deliveries. Sections envision the space and show the proportion of the raised beds. Vining plants grow on overhead metal structures, which provide an opportunity for Magdiale to incorporate art into the garden—whimsical or modern sculptural pieces with one end centered in one of the beds for cordoned apple trees (trained as a single, ropelike stem) or climbing vines, and the other end attached directly to the building. This forms a space for customers and the chef to walk through, where dangling apples or bitter melons might hang.

Planting design

I created a specific planting design (1 in. = 2 ft. so that the spacing of individual plants could be noted), which was determined by the availability of organic seed for each variety. Many types of certified organic seeds are readily available from seed catalogs.

'Scarlet Emperor' runner bean will climb the lattice fence on the west side of the garden, creating a sense of enclosure with living green walls, while producing edible flowers and pods. 'Dow Purple Pod' snap bean will climb the wooden fence; this rare heirloom produces flat purple pods. The six jostaberry trees lined up in the raised beds create a rhythm as one enters the garden from the west gate. Jostaberry, a cross between a gooseberry and a black currant, can be trained as a *standard*—a shrub shaped like a tree, with a single stem. This ornamental plant has unusual black fruits for tarts, jams, or pies. (Some states prohibit the cultivation of currant because it is an alternate host to white pine blister rust. However, no white pines are within the vicinity and since this a disease-resistant cultivar, this is not a problem.)

The plan leaves ample room for lettuces and greens such as tatsoi that can be seeded repeatedly for a continuous harvest. These can be plucked at any stage, from tender new sprouts to full-size leaves. Choosing cool- and warm-season varieties allows lettuce to be grown throughout the season. Asparagus is a perennial that produces ferny foliage up to 6 ft. (2 m) tall.

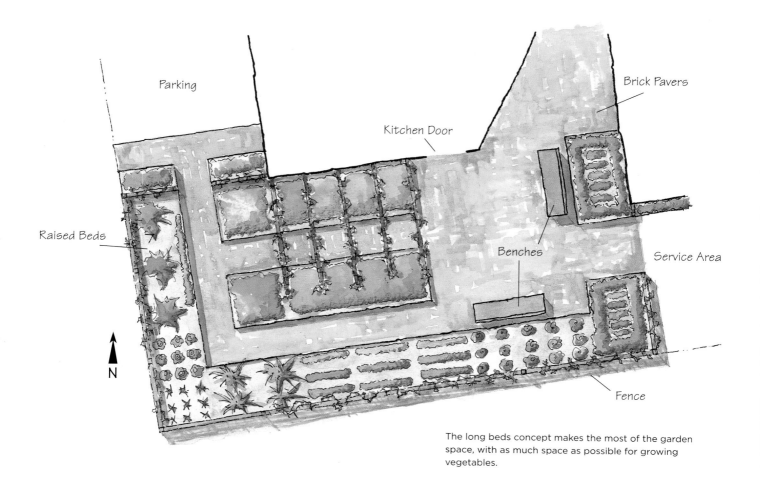

Parking

Kitchen Door

Brick Pavers

Raised Beds

Benches

Service Area

Fence

N

The long beds concept makes the most of the garden space, with as much space as possible for growing vegetables.

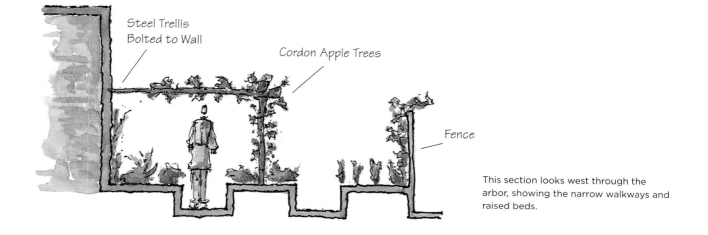

Steel Trellis Bolted to Wall

Cordon Apple Trees

Fence

This section looks west through the arbor, showing the narrow walkways and raised beds.

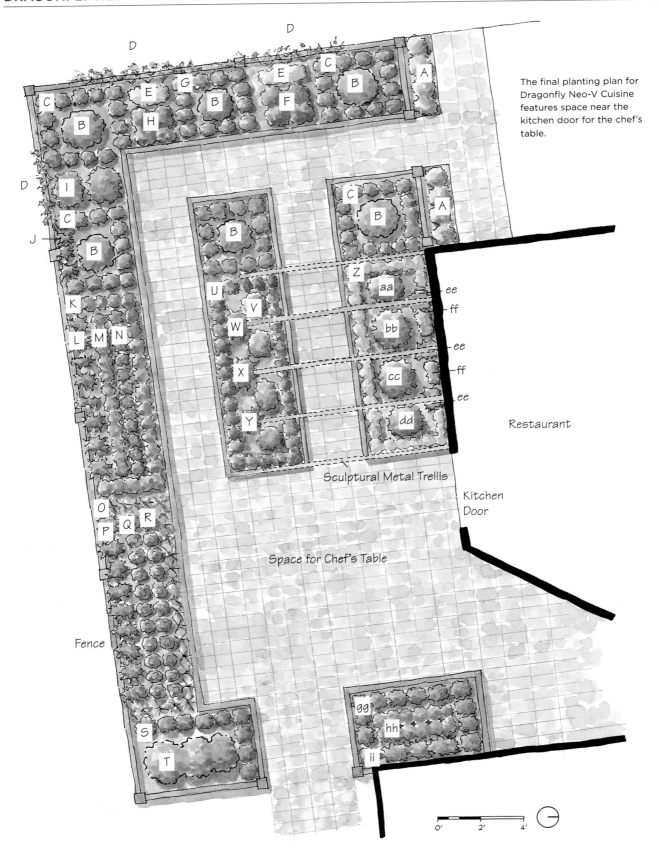

The final planting plan for Dragonfly Neo-V Cuisine features space near the kitchen door for the chef's table.

Restaurant

Kitchen Door

Sculptural Metal Trellis

Space for Chef's Table

Fence

0' 2' 4'

Key

LABEL	COMMON NAME	SCIENTIFIC NAME	NO. OF PLANTS	LIFE CYCLE	COMMENTS
A	Jerusalem artichoke	*Helianthus tuberosus* 'Stampede'	8	perennial, Zones 3–9	yellow flowers, grown for edible white tubers
B	jostaberry	*Ribes nidigrolaria*	6	deciduous, Zones 3–8	shrub, cross between black currant and gooseberry
C	'Gigante d'Italia' parsley	*Petroselinum crispum* 'Gigante d'Italia'	47	biennial, Zone 5	plant flat leaf heirloom as an annual
D	scarlet runner bean	*Phaseolus coccineus* 'Scarlet Emperor'	16	annual	vigorous climber with edible flowers and pods
E	'Lemon Gem' signet marigold	*Tagetes signata* 'Lemon Gem'	6	annual	lemon-scented edible flowers
F	anise hyssop	*Agastache foeniculum*	4	perennial, Zones 4–9	leaves and flowers make an anise-flavored tea
G	cilantro	*Coriandrum sativum*	24	annual	fresh leaves known as *cilantro*, dried seeds known as *coriander*
H	'Osaka Purple' mustard	*Brassica juncea* 'Osaka Purple'	4	annual	cool season crop but bolt-resistant in the heat, with large, pungent purple leaves
I	'Yukon Gold' potato	*Solanum tuberosum* 'Yukon Gold'	2	tuber	early season small potato with yellow flesh
J	'Dow Purple Pod' snap bean	*Phaseolus vulgaris* 'Dow Purple Pod'	3	annual	heirloom producing flat, purple pods
K	'Lolla Rossa' lettuce	*Lactuca sativa* 'Lolla Rossa'	21	annual	red frilly leaves, seed every three weeks
L	'Garden of Eden' climbing bean	*Phaseolus vulgaris* 'Garden of Eden'	8	annual	heirloom pole bean
M	'Lettuce Leaf' basil	*Ocimum basilicum* 'Lettuce Leaf'	12	annual	large leaves and edible flowers
N	'Genovese' basil	*Ocimum basilicum* 'Genovese'	12	annual	classic pesto basil
O	'King Richard' leek	*Allium ampeloprasum* 'King Richard'	24	biennial	grown as an annual; early, with long, slender shanks
P	'Blauhilde' climbing bean	*Phaseolus vulgaris* 'Blauhilde'	9	annual	fence climber has purple pods that turn green when cooked
Q	'Merveille des Quatre Saisons' lettuce	*Lactuca sativa* 'Merveille des Quatre Saisons'	11	annual	butterhead with red-tinged leaves
R	'Merlot' lettuce	*Lactuca sativa* 'Merlot'	11	annual	red leaves perfect for "cut and come again"
S	mizuna	*Brassica rapa* (Japonica Group)	9	annual	easy to grow, mild flavor
T	'Jersey King' asparagus	*Asparagus officinalis* 'Jersey King'	3	perennial, Zone 4	three to five years for maximum productivity, with baby asparagus every spring
U	thyme	*Thymus vulgaris*	32	perennial, Zones 5–9	use fresh in sauces
V	'Violetta Lunga Precoce' eggplant	*Solanum melongena* 'Violetta Lunga Precoce'	4	annual	long, narrow, purple eggplant with classic taste
W	'Red Boskop' apple	*Malus* 'Red Boskop'	1	deciduous tree	grow as small cordon on metal structure
X	'Chehalis' apple	*Malus* 'Chehalis'	1	deciduous tree	grow as small cordon on metal structure
Y	'William's Pride' apple	*Malus* 'William's Pride'	1	deciduous tree	grow as small cordon on metal structure
Z	'Radio' calendula	*Calendula officinalis* 'Radio'	26	annual	heirloom from 1930s with bright orange edible flowers
aa	'Green Zebra' tomato	*Solanum lycopersicum* 'Green Zebra'	1	annual	green tomato
bb	'Taxi' tomato	*Solanum lycopersicum* 'Taxi'	1	annual	sweet yellow determinate tomato

(continued from previous page)

LABEL	COMMON NAME	SCIENTIFIC NAME	NO. OF PLANTS	LIFE CYCLE	COMMENTS
cc	'Debarao' tomato	*Solanum lycopersicum* 'Debarao'	1	annual	heirloom small, red variety good for sauces
dd	'White Beauty' tomato	*Solanum lycopersicum* 'White Beauty'	1	annual	large, white beefsteak
ee	dill	*Anethum graveolens*	9	annual	grown for leaf and seeds
ff	rosemary	*Rosmarinus officinalis*	4	perennial, Zones 7–10	grow as an annual, leaves good in foccacia
gg	'Deer Tongue' lettuce	*Lactuca sativa* 'Deer Tongue'	12	annual	heirloom green bibb lettuce
hh	tatsoi greens	*Brassica rapa* 'Tatsoi'	12	annual	cool season, compact rosette with mild taste
ii	'Goldmarie Vining' bean	*Phaseolus vulgaris* 'Goldmarie Vining'	3	annual	climber has flat yellow pods

THE BARTLEY POTAGER
A suburban residential potager

My potager evolved over many years but began with a primary goal: to create a special place to grow herbs and vegetables that I use on a daily basis. Now it is a focal point of summer days and outdoor meals. It is easy to set up a small table in the center of the garden, inside the picket fence, over the small central diamond of low-growing silver thyme. Our most intimate meals are eaten within the small enclosure, surrounded by the growing vines, flowers, and tomatoes, but most often guests are served on the deck that overlooks the potager.

Layout and placement

My potager is on the east side of our house and receives at least six hours of morning and afternoon sun. By late afternoon, the garden begins to be shaded by the house, but I have had great success with growing sun-loving vegetables and flowers. The cobalt blue trellises match the wall color of my dining room, so the beauty of the kitchen garden extends into the house. Since the garden is adjacent to the house, I do not have to imagine how the plants are doing when I'm not outside—I can enjoy the lushness from the views through the inside windows.

The potager runs the length of the house, with each end in line with the building's edges. I created a pleasing rectangular planting on the east side of the house—away from the house a bit, but this site provides as much opportunity as possible for sun exposure, within the framework of the design. The layout is a traditional quadripartite form with four raised wood-sided beds. After a friend with a backhoe excavated the 30 by 40 ft.

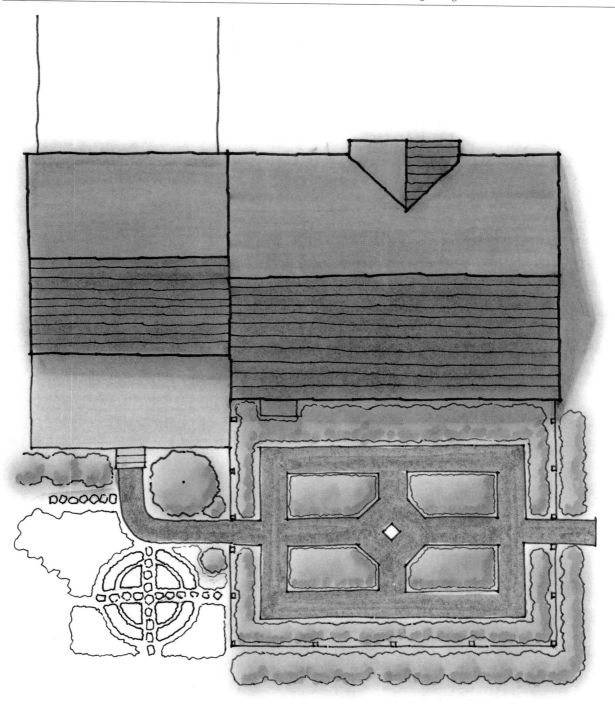

The relationship of the Bartley potager to the house; the garden is on the east side, where it receives ample light.

An isometric view of the Bartley Potager shows planting beds and the fence with plantings.

Key

LABEL	COMMON NAME	SCIENTIFIC NAME	NO. OF PLANTS	LIFE CYCLE	HARDINESS ZONE	COMMENTS
A	hydrangea	*Hydrangea macrophylla* 'Endless Summer'	6	deciduous shrub	4	
B	yew	*Taxus ×media* 'Brownii'	7	evergreen shrub	4	provides green color year-round
C	boxwood	*Buxus* 'Green Gem'	16	evergreen shrub	4	adds winter interest
D	thyme	*Thymus vulgaris*	40	perennial	5	
E	maiden grass	*Miscanthus sinensis* 'Gracillimus'	4	perennial	5	
F	highbush blueberry	*Vaccinium corymbosum* 'Blueray'	10	deciduous shrub	3	good fall color
G	peony	*Paeonia* 'Sarah Bernhardt'	11	perennial	2	fragrant, double pink variety dates to 1906
H	strawberry	*Fragaria ×ananassa* 'Redchief'	40	perennial		

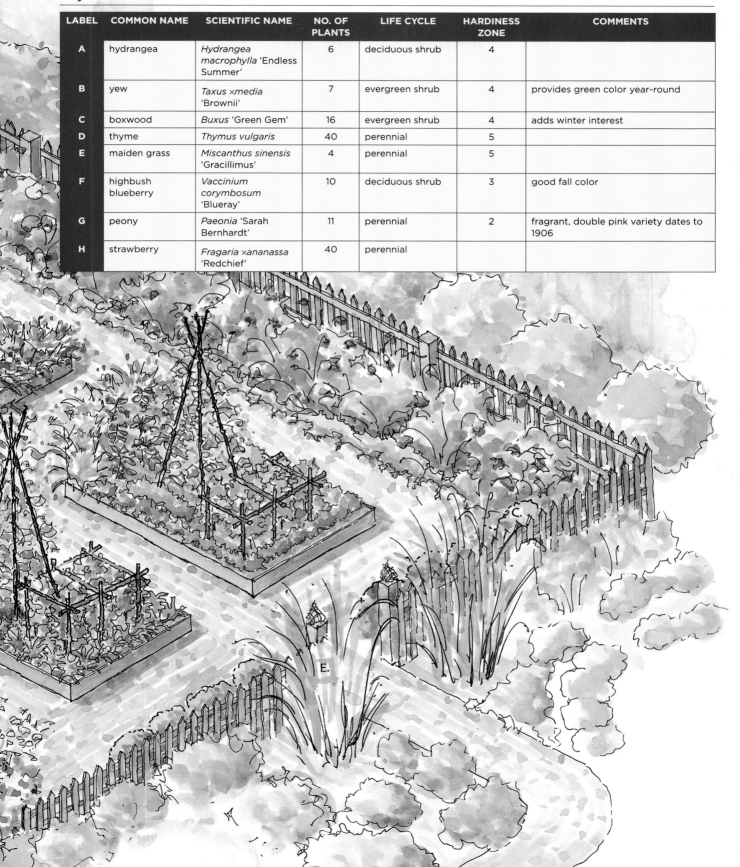

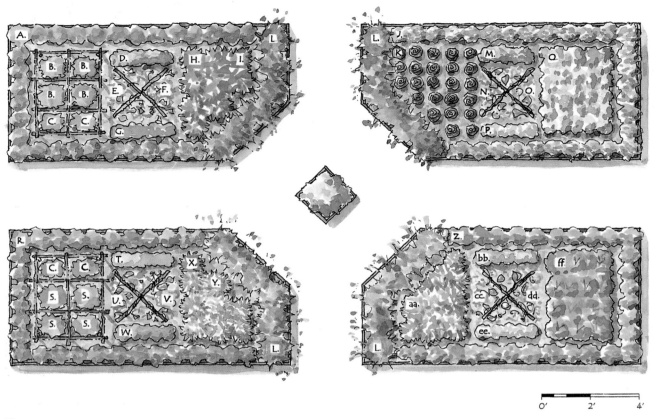

Key

LABEL	COMMON NAME	SCIENTIFIC NAME	NO. OF PLANTS	LIFE CYCLE	COMMENTS
A	black palm cabbage	*Brassica oleracea* 'Nero Di Toscana'	29	annual	fan-shaped blue-green heirloom kale
B	'Purple Russian' heirloom tomato	*Solanum lycopersicum* 'Purple Russian'	4	annual	sweet purple and red fist-size tomato, highly recommended
C	'Principe Borghese' heirloom tomato	*Solanum lycopersicum* 'Principe Borghese'	4	annual	Italian plum tomato for paste or drying
D	violet	*Viola* 'Etain'	4	perennial, Zones 4–8	used as an annual, favors cool weather, and fragrant
E	scarlet emperor runner bean	*Phaseollus coccineus* 'Scarlet Emperor'	12	annual	bright red edible flowers of good climber attract hummingbirds
F	'Heavenly Blue' morning glory	*Ipomoea tricolor* 'Heavenly Blue'	4	annual	color is stunning on trellises and fences, but plant is poisonous
G	lavender cotton	*Santolina chamaecyparissus*	4	perennial, Zones 6–8	use as an annual, with fragrant gray-green leaves
H	'Sweet Genovese' basil	*Ocimum basilicum* 'Sweet Genovese'	8	annual	classic basil for pesto
I	lime basil	*Ocimum americanum* 'Lime'	2	annual	lime-flavored basil
J	'Empress of India' nasturtiums	*Tropaeolum majus* 'Empress of India'	29	annual	edible orange-red flowers with blue-green foliage
K	lettuce mix			annual	seed every two weeks, thin, then cut and come again

LABEL	COMMON NAME	SCIENTIFIC NAME	NO. OF PLANTS	LIFE CYCLE	COMMENTS
L	lavender	*Lavandula angustifolia* 'Munstead'	24	perennial	
M	rosemary	*Rosmarinus officinalis* 'Hardy Hill'	4	perennial, Zones 7–10	might survive Zone 6 with protection; in Zone 5 use as an annual
N	'Emerite' pole beans	*Phaseollus vulgaris* 'Emerite'	12	annual	tender French bean, highly recommended
O	bitter melon	*Momordica charantia*	4	annual	difficult to germinate
P	lavender cotton	*Santolina chamaecyparissus*	4	perennial, Zones 6–8	used as an annual with fragrant gray-green leaves
Q	'Bull's Blood' beet	*Beta vulgaris* 'Bull's Blood'	25	annual	deep red leaves are edible, beets best when small
R	Italian parsley	*Petroselinum crispum* 'Giant of Italy'	29	biennial	classic flat leaf parsley with long-season green color and good flavor
S	'Orange Banana' heirloom tomato	*Solanum lycopersicum* 'Orange Banana'	4	annual	sweet orange tomato with a taste of kiwi, highly recommended
T	'Bon Bon Orange' calendula	*Calendua officinalis* 'Bon Bon Orange'	4	annual	bright orange flowers are edible
U	miniature pumpkin	*Cucurbita pepo* 'Jack Be Little'	4	annual	train mini pumpkins on tepees
V	'Heavenly Blue' morning glory	*Ipomoea tricolor* 'Heavenly Blue'	8	annual	
W	tatsoi	*Brassica rapa* 'Tatsoi'	6	annual	thrives in cool weather, and leaves can be cut and will regrow
X	'Cinnamon' basil	*Ocimum basilicum* 'Cinnamon'	4	annual	violet red stems and veins
Y	'Ebony Wonder' basil	*Ocimum basilicum* 'Ebony Wonder'	5	tender	dark purple leaves and pink edible flowers
Z	'Bambino' eggplant	*Solanum melongea* 'Bambino'	29	annual	
aa	bull's horn sweet pepper	*Capsicum annuum* 'Corno di Toro Rosso'	9	annual	mild pepper can be eaten green or when red, highly recommended
bb	yellow calendula	*Calendula officinalis*	5	annual	from an old garden, a true yellow edible flower
cc	hyacinth bean	*Dolichos lablab*	12	annual	inedible vigorous climber with lavender flowers and purple pods
dd	'Heavenly Blue' morning glory	*Ipomoea tricolor* 'Heavenly Blue'	4	annual	poisonous striking blue flowers
ee	white marigold	*Tagetes erecta* 'Sweet Cream'	5	annual	
ff	'Bright Lights' Swiss chard	*Beta vulgaris* 'Bright Lights'	16	annual	colorful leafy addition to the garden

(9 by 12 m) rectangle, we filled it with crushed gravel for the base. We built four wooden boxes and placed them over the tamped crushed gravel, with an ample 3 ft. (1 m) walkway between them. The beds edge the brick in the center of the garden and one side of the outer walk. We laid brick on the base in a running bond pattern, using a plastic edge to hold the last row of bricks in place. We swept sand into the cracks between bricks.

A gothic picket fence with simple pointed pickets surrounds the garden. Entrance to the garden is from the north or the south, as entry gates with ball and chain closures create a passageway through the garden. Two

Miscanthus sinensis 'Gracillimus' flank the entry into the garden, standing like green pillars on each side of the gate.

We attached a wire fence with small openings to the outside lower half of the fence, which is practically invisible from the house and in the potager, as carefully placed plantings hide it. The wire fence is a couple of inches below the soil line and does an excellent job of keeping out the rabbits, which boldly romp in all other places in the yard.

Planting plan

A row of highbush blueberries planted just outside the potager fence provides an edible part of the layered enclosure. Blueberries are an excellent choice for the residential landscape because they are attractive in many seasons, even if the birds enjoy more fruit than we do. In the spring, white blossoms appear, followed by blueberries in the summer. In the fall, the leaves turn a deep red.

Heirloom peonies from my grandmother's farm are planted just inside the picket fence. Although the peonies are wonderful in the spring, as the season progresses their attractiveness in the border wanes, with their green foliage turning to brown by late fall. Nevertheless, the spectacular impact of multiple-blooming fragrant peony varieties makes them valuable in the potager for fragrance, color, and cut flowers. Peonies also attract beneficial insects to the garden.

Heirloom peonies grow with borage along the fence in my potager. Edible *Borago officinalis* and ornamental *Paeonia officinalis* also grew in medieval monastery gardens.

Strawberries are planted as an edible ground cover under the peonies. The everblooming variety produces abundantly in the spring and then sporadically through the season. In the fall and winter, the leaves turn burgundy red. Boxwood is planted in rows on each side of the gates at the north and south ends of the garden, creating a formal symmetry to the potager in addition to winter color.

Lavender is planted in each of the four central raised beds. This perennial herb from the Mediterranean prefers drier conditions than the vegetables growing nearby. Because I water by hand, selective watering is not a problem—I simply use more water for the peppers and other plants and less for the lavender. The fragrant herb flowers all season and the blooms spill over onto the brick walkway. The remainder of the space in the four beds is reserved for annuals, which are selected based on new varieties I want to try and old favorites rotated on a four-year cycle. Perennial herbs such as thyme, mint, and oregano are relegated to a small space just outside the fence, between the outdoor deck and enclosed garden. This is a result of too small a space and too large an appetite for more peppers, tomatoes, greens, and beans.

Green is a color of winter when boxwood or other evergreens are planted in the potager.

A RESIDENTIAL SHADE GARDEN

In many older neighborhoods, mature trees block the sunny conditions necessary to grow some vegetables. Some edible plants do tolerate shade, though, and some even prefer this condition. Though each plant has its own particular best growing conditions, in general vegetables grown for their fruits need full sun and vegetables and herbs grown for their leaves and roots can tolerate some shade.

I designed a part-sun residential potager for a client who wanted a small gathering space for her teenage sons to sit and play guitar in the summer evenings. She also wanted a small plot that provided some space for either vegetables or flowers, depending on her mood at the time of spring planting. The ideal place for this edible garden was on the east side of her house. This would usually be a good location for morning sun, but mature

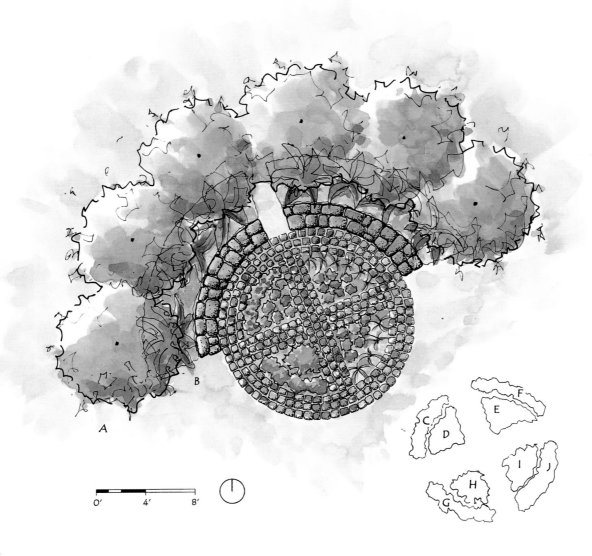

0'   4'   8'

Key

LABEL	COMMON NAME	SCIENTIFIC NAME	NO. OF PLANTS	HABIT	COMMENTS
A	paw paw	*Asimina triloba*	6	understory tree	fruit is green-yellow and custardlike
B	ostrich fern	*Matteuccia struthiopteris*	8	perennial, Zones 2–8	fiddle heads are edible
C	Johnny-jump-up	*Viola tricolor*	6	annual	heirloom purple and yellow edible flowers
D	'D'Etampes' mâche	*Valerianella locusta* 'D'Etampes'		annual	seed in early spring then in succession throughout the season
E	mizuna	*Brassica rapa* (Japonica Group)		use as annual	heat- and cold-tolerant mustard reseeds for continual harvest
F	'New York White' garlic	*Allium sativum* 'New York White'	16	bulb	plant bulbs in fall; harvest half when young the rest in midsummer

An isometric view of the edible shade garden shows the stone seat wall and paw paw trees.

LABEL	COMMON NAME	SCIENTIFIC NAME	NO. OF PLANTS	HABIT	COMMENTS
G	'Chioggia' beet	*Beta vulgaris* 'Chioggia'	5	annual	heirloom Italian variety has red and white rings and red skin
H	'Zefa Fino' fennel	*Foeniculum vulgare* 'Zefa Fino'	3	use as annual	Italian variety bulb fennel
I	'Fordhook Giant' Swiss chard	*Beta vulgaris* (Cicla Group)	5	annual	large green leaves with white stems
J	'King Richard' leek	*Allium ampeloprasum* 'King Richard'	12	annual	vertical beauty good for baby leeks

pine trees at the rear of her small yard cast a shadow over the lawn, and the Zone 5 garden received only about three to four hours of sunlight a day.

The client enjoys drinking her morning coffee on the outdoor deck that overlooks her backyard. We planned the potager to be built on a direct axis with the sliding door leading to the deck. This garden is now the central focal point of her property, and she enjoys gazing at the growing produce or sitting in the midst of it. Her sons, who are strict vegetarians, also enjoy the simplicity of preparing meals from the garden when they are home from college.

Paw paw trees are planted along the edge of the garden. Paw paws have a tap root and prefer shady conditions. These understory trees once grew prolifically in the virgin forests of the southern and midwestern parts of the United States. I remember harvesting paw paws in the ravine behind our house and helping my father make paw paw wine. Native Americans also harvested the oval, yellow-green fruit, which is similar to a banana in texture. The tree is also host to the eggs of the zebra swallowtail butterfly.

Ostrich ferns were placed behind the stone seat wall to create a nice backdrop. Paired with the paw paw trees, they make a comfortable space for sitting in the garden. The ostrich fern prefers moist, rich soil in part shade and can reach about 4 ft. (1 m) in height. The tiny fronds begin to unfold in the early spring. When the fronds are green and tightly wound (called *crosiers*), they can be picked and cooked as a delicacy, a traditional spring treat in Canada and the U.S. Northeast. After the crosiers are thoroughly washed, they must be boiled for at least 10 minutes before being added to a sauté or stew for additional cooking. The ostrich fern is a perennial and will produce fiddleheads followed by lush fronds.

'Zefa Fino' fennel is a bulbing fennel, called *finnochio* in Italy. The white leaf stalks swell to produce the layered vegetable. Bulb fennel has a mild anise flavor and can be used raw in salads or braised, grilled, or sautéed. The airy foliage is also aromatic and great for salads and flavoring. Herb fennel looks similar to the bulbing type but does not produce the swollen stalks and is allowed to flower. Bulb fennel is planted in midsummer for a fall harvest, while herb fennel is planted in the early spring for long-season foliage that attracts beneficial insects.

A PERENNIAL EDIBLE GARDEN

There is such a thing as a low-maintenance vegetable garden. Most vegetables and many flowers in the potager are annuals that need to be planted yearly and the beds maintained to support each new crop. Perennial vegetables, herbs, and flowers, which maintain a permanent place in the garden, may require less time in yearly preparation and maintenance. However, some chores do need to be done: weeding, mulching, fertilizing, and watering are still necessary to maintain an enjoyable, healthy perennial garden.

This design for a lower maintenance potager includes fresh herbs, edible and decorative flowers, and vegetables throughout the season. The plan shows no annual vegetables, but small spaces could be made for easily sown annual herbs such as dill, cilantro, and fennel. Little niches could be created for easy-to-grow vegetables such as chard, beets, or radishes. These would serve as colorful punctuations in the garden. One single 'Bright Lights' Swiss chard with its bright red stems and green leaves would contrast well with the limey green of a chamaecyparis.

This pass-through space is on the south side of the house, but the design could be adapted to a front entry or backyard, depending on the aspect of the garden. This potager garden will receive ample sunlight throughout the day. The 3 ft. (1 m) pathway is made of crushed gravel that is hard packed and wide enough for a wheelbarrow. The space is large enough to grow two perennial favorites: asparagus and rhubarb, which need ample room. In the spring, the garden will supply asparagus for the dinner plate, followed by blooms of peony to decorate the table.

'Russelliana' rose is a fragrant pink climbing rose, and 'Darlow's Enigma' is a fragrant white climbing rose. Both are hardy in Zone 5 and grow on their own root stock. Planted behind the fence is a row of everbearing red raspberries. 'Summit' can be cut to the ground every spring and will produce a crop in late summer. This simplifies the pruning of canes and will help keep the row neat and manageable.

Two plum trees are also planted in the garden; both are European plums and are hardy in Zones 5 to 9. The eventual height of the plum tree depends on the root stock to which the fruit tree is grafted. In this situation, a small 12 to 15 ft. (3.5 to 4.5 m) tree is suitable. 'Italian Prune' is one of the Fellenburg plum types from Germany and is self-fertile. The fruits are dark purple and suitable for desserts or drying. 'Bavay's Green Gage' is originally from Belgium and is also self-fertile. These varieties are recommended for the climate zones of the American Midwest.

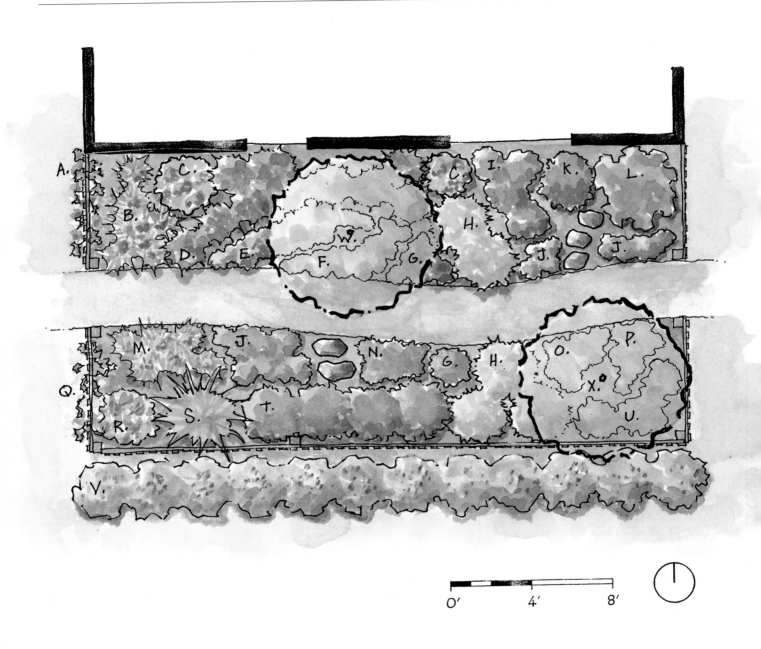

0'   4'   8'

The plan view of the perennial edible garden on the south side of the residence.

Key

LABEL	COMMON NAME	SCIENTIFIC NAME	NO. OF PLANTS	HARDINESS ZONES	COMMENTS
A	'Russelliana' climbing rose	*Rosa* 'Russelliana'	1	5–9	*Russelliana* HMult prior to 1837
B	daylilly	*Hemerocallis* 'Strawberry Candy'	7	3–10	
C	peony	*Paeonia lactiflora* 'Raspberry Sundae'	2	2–10	
D	lavender	*Lavandula angustifolia* 'Rosea'	10	5–9	pink flowers, grows to 15 in.
E	silver thyme	*Thymus vulgaris* 'Argenteus'	11	5–9	culinary thyme with silver leaves
F	'Doone Valley' thyme	*Thymus ×citriodorus* 'Doone Valley'	11	5–9	pale lilac flowers have lemon scent and flavor, grows to 12 in.
G	purple sage	*Salvia officinalis* 'Purpurascens'	8	4–8	purple foliage, grows to 24 in.
H	dwarf Japanese false cypress	*Chamaecyparis pisifera* 'Sungold'	5	4–8	provides year-round interest, with bright yellow new growth
I	hyssop	*Agastache foeniculum*	4	5–9	24–36 in. purple flowers good for tea, attracts bees
J	chives	*Allium schoenophrasum*	16	3–9	pink edible flowers and leaves
K	borage	*Borago officinalis*	1	annual	purple, drooping edible flowers attract bees, readily self-seeds
L	rhubarb	*Rheum rhabarbarum* 'Cherry Red'	1	3–7	bright red leafstalk with inedible leaves and 15–20 year life span
M	daylilly	*Hemerocallis* 'Lullaby Baby'	6	3–10	pale pink, grows to 20 in.
N	catmint	*Nepeta mussinii* 'Blue Wonder'	5	3–10	bright blue flowers on 18 in. plants
O	Greek oregano	*Oreganum vulgare* subsp. *hirtum*	7	5–10	True spicy Greek oregano grows to 12–18 in.
P	golden sage	*Salvia officinalis* 'Aurea'	7	5–9	bold, gold, variegated leaves for culinary use
Q	'Darlow's Enigma' climbing rose	*Rosa* 'Darlow's Enigma'	1	5–9	fragrant white climber
R	contorted quince	*Chaenomeles speciosa*	1		pink flowers on 2–3 ft. shrub, striking in winter
S	silver variegated maiden grass	*Miscanthus sinensis* 'Morning Light'	1		grows 5 by 3 ft.
T	asparagus	*Asparagus officinalis* 'Jersey King'	4		improved hybrid resists rust and fusarium, predominance of male plants
U	Japanese parsley	*Cryptotaenia japonica* f. *atropurpurea*	3		perennial, grows to 4 ft.; new leaves chopped for salads and stir fry
V	everbearing red raspberry	*Rubus idaeus* 'Heritage'	12	3–9	no trellis needed; prune a few inches above ground each winter, produces crop in late summer
W	'Bavay's Green Gage' plum	*Prunus domestica* 'Bavay's Green Gage'	1	5–9	old self-fertile variety with sweet fruit
X	'Italian Prune' plum tree	*Prunus domestica* 'Italian Prune'	1	5–9	large self-fertile variety with purple fruit

When we run out of room in the formal potager to grow everything we desire, we can fill containers with vegetables, herbs, and a mix of edible and inedible flowers.

CONTAINER POTAGER GARDENING

Often times, a small planned potager doesn't afford enough room to grow every herb, vegetable, and fruit we desire. Placing edibles in containers expands the palette of choices and adds color, texture, variety, and beauty to an otherwise barren spot. Container gardening also allows us to give in to the inevitable temptation to try new varieties from the nursery—lime basil or 'Peach Melba' nasturtiums with blue bachelor's buttons. Perennials can be planted in the container garden as well. Sage does well and revives every spring after overwintering in a garage. Or bring it inside for fresh leaves for the Thanksgiving turkey. Mint belongs in containers, which keeps it from spreading throughout the rest of the garden.

By planting in containers, we can increase the variety of plants contributing to the overall diversity of the garden. For example, bronze fennel, with its airy, fernlike, edible leaves, takes up an entire pot to attract butterflies and beneficial insect predators to the garden.

This assortment of pots along the fence offers flexible options to expand the potager. The arrangement is temporary, as clay pots in climate Zone 5 must be emptied of soil and turned upside down at the end of the season or stored in the garage where they will not freeze. So the grouping of edible and inedible plants is changed yearly based on the gardener's whim and desire. The pots can also be moved during the season for special occasions in the garden.

Early in the season, a bold cardoon is grown with nasturtiums and other herbs and flowers just outside the potager fence. A variety of plants, such as bronze fennel, help attract beneficial insects to the garden.

CHAPTER EIGHT

Building and Maintaining the Edible Garden

GROWING YOUR OWN VEGETABLES AND FLOWERS from seed is easy and rewarding. It extends the enjoyment and pleasure of the kitchen garden as you dream, plan, order your seeds, and plant them. Unless you have an arrangement with a nearby nursery, planting your own seeds is the only way to grow specialty heirloom varieties and ensure that they are grown organically. (Many nurseries just can't make the commitment to growing chemical-free.) Growing your own seedlings is less expensive than buying plants, but it does require more patience. The rewards are great, however, for we expand the lessons that the garden teaches us. What better way to spend a February day than nurturing a tiny green sprout, ensuring the small baby has all it needs to flourish? Can it be that the healing nature of the garden begins here as we focus on life?

In the potager, the emphasis is on experimentation and diversity, not rows and rows of the same vegetable variety. Many seeds will remain viable for a few years, if not longer (check the seed packet). Start a few seeds of many varieties to see how you like them and how they grow in your garden; then store the rest of the seeds to use the next year. Or you can share the varieties of plants you grow with a friend who also starts his or her own seedlings.

ORDERING SEED

Select the seed varieties you plant based on taste and beauty and a sense of adventure. Looking through catalogs can be like shopping in a candy store, with many colors and varieties from which to choose. Seed catalogs are a tremendous resource for gathering information on each plant's best chance for survival in your garden. A plethora of catalogs offer heirloom and organic seed varieties. Look through the "Seed and Fruit Sources" list near the end of the book to get started. An understanding of some common definitions will help you navigate through seed catalog descriptions as you plan your garden.

Perennials

Perennial plants return season after season without replanting. The gardener does the work of planting one year and enjoys the rewards for many. Some perennials, such as peonies, rhubarb, and asparagus, last many years in the garden. Others languish with time and should be replaced after three or four years, such as thyme and lavender, which become woody as they age. Perennials have individual growing requirements that ensure their ability to thrive. One of the major classifications is the plant's hardiness zone, which reflects its cold tolerance. This is a general indicator of the survivability of the plant in your region.

Plant perennials in a place where their roots will not be disturbed in the kitchen garden. Traditionally, medicinal perennial herbs were planted in beds separate from the annual vegetables, but perennials can be used as edging plants in the potager; just don't disturb the plant roots as you maintain the rest of the bed. In the American Midwest, rosemary, santolina, and some of the sages, thymes, and lavender varieties are not hardy. These plants are planted in spring and brought into the greenhouse or house for the winter.

Annuals

Annual plants complete their life cycle in one season: they sprout, flower, produce seed, and then die. Annuals must be replanted every year. Some annuals easily reseed and come up on their own, all over the garden. Dill and borage seeds can drift around the garden, sprouting in unexpected places. Dill takes up little space, and young plants can be harvested and used in the kitchen. Borage, however, is more problematic; the large, hairy leaves take up a lot of room. Borage has its permanent place in the garden because of its intense blue edible flowers and should have its own special spot in which to reseed. Dill is allowed to roam in my garden, but borage seedlings that randomly sprout in unexpected places are removed. To prevent annuals and some perennials from appearing in unwanted spots around the garden, remove the plants' seed heads or cut the flowers before they go to seed.

Biennials

Biennials complete their life cycle over two seasons, growing the first season and producing flowers and seeds the second. Most of the root crops, including beets, carrots, parsnips, and rutabaga, are biennials. Parsley, cabbage, leeks, onions, kohlrabi, brussels sprouts, and celery are biennials. Leeks and parsnips, and once in a while parsley, may overwinter in the garden, as they are sometimes hardy to -20° F (-29° C), but other plants must be dug up in the fall, stored in a cool place, and then replanted in the spring so they can flower. Most often, these plants are treated as annuals—grown from seed, planted, and harvested yearly.

Organic

Organic gardening is a popular theme. Even in grocery stores, many foods are labeled "Certified organic." What do the words mean and what does it mean to grow organically? Since 2002, the United States Department of Agriculture requires that a set of standards must be met before food products can bear the certified organic label. This is important information for the gardener who wants to use organic seed.

The chef who desires that her potager garden be certified as organic and the market gardener using the label must have their gardens inspected by a state representative of the USDA. It is not necessary for the home gardener to go through all the paperwork to meet the certification, but understanding the government's definition is helpful. In general, to receive a USDA certified organic label, produce must have been grown from seed without the use of chemical pesticides or fertilizers made from synthetic materials or sewage sludge, arsenate treated wood products must not have been used for planting beds or trellises, and the garden must have been inspected and must maintain documentation certifying compliance. Small farmers grossing less than $5000 a year are exempt from certification fees but can label their crops organic only if they comply with the requirements.

Organic gardening in the home potager means growing in connection with nature by minimizing the use of synthetic fertilizers derived from oil by-products and choosing fertilizers originating from renewable sources. It means not using synthetic pesticides and fungicides to kill harmful and beneficial insects, and instead using mechanical means (hand picking) or benign products to remove pests selectively. It means building the soil and planting a variety of plants to attract beneficial insects to the garden. For the cook and gardener, growing organic means tasting sugar snap peas and cherry tomatoes off the vine with complete confidence that you're eating nothing but fresh, pure vegetables.

Heirloom varieties

Opinions differ as to what, exactly, is an heirloom variety fruit or vegetable, but in general, heirlooms are open-pollinated varieties (not hybrids) that have been passed down through generations because of desirable characteristics. All heirloom plants are open-pollinated, but not all open-pollinated plants are heirloom. Seed Savers Exchange, a nonprofit organization dedicated to preserving heirloom varieties, defines an heirloom on the organization's website (www.seedsavers.org) as "any garden plant that has a history of being passed down within a family, just like pieces of heirloom jewelry or furniture." At one time, saving seeds from one year was the only way a family could ensure they'd have enough food to eat the following year. These seeds became precious links to life, and eating a special tomato recounted the family's history. Saving the seed carried on the tradition.

Seeds are not commonly handed down to children today. I treasure the peonies from my grandparents' farm and the memory of the vegetables they grew, not the genetics of the tomatoes and beans. But saving seed is a tradition we can begin anew, and this practice is growing in popularity among gardeners. Planting a garden today and saving some of the seed will demonstrate to our children the value of plants and the importance of preservation.

Seed Savers Exchange is devoted to saving genetically diverse seeds from extinction. More than 24,000 rare vegetable varieties are being permanently maintained at the organization's farm. Ten percent of the seeds are planted yearly on a 10-year crop rotation cycle. Membership in the exchange allows gardeners to access others who are saving seeds and supports the cause of preserving the wealth of diversity in the genetics of the plants. Preservation of remaining rare varieties is crucial, because once a variety becomes extinct, its unique characteristics are gone forever—they cannot be duplicated. Growing heirloom varieties promotes genetic diversity, even if you do not continue to save your own seed. When you buy from those who are saving rare varieties, you are ensuring a healthy and diverse plant resource for future generations.

Look to heirlooms such as these for specialty varieties and taste: Red-seeded asparagus bean is a Chinese heirloom that produces dark red, stringless beans that are 2 ft. (61 cm) long. 'Cosmic Purple' carrots have bright purple skin with yellow to orange flesh. Thomas Jefferson grew the fragrant green heirloom melon 'Ananas D'Amerique a Chair Verte' in his garden. Heirloom tomatoes come in a variety of colors, including white, purple, green, yellow, orange, and red. Heirloom peppers are purple, green, red, white, chocolate brown, and orange and range in size, shape, and heat.

Hybrids

In the context of vegetable breeding, a hybrid is a cross between two distinct varieties of the same species. Plant breeders look for positive characteristics in plants they want to cross, and the process of isolating that gene can be lengthy. It takes time to grow a number of generations of plants, inspecting the progeny and crossing again until the desired gene is stabilized. Each parent variety has different genetic material and may have been bred for that characteristic over a long period of time. One parent plant may have vibrant color, while another may have high disease resistance. When crossed, the first generation result is called an *F1 hybrid*—the new plant has the characteristics of both parent plants. Because this new plant will not produce seeds true to type, there is no reason to save these seeds—the plants will revert to the parent plants or their lineage with unknown results. Hybrid seed is manufactured to assure reliability in the desired traits.

Open-pollinated plants

Open-pollinated plants will produce offspring with the same characteristics of the parent plant—called *true to type*—if they are isolated from other varieties of the same species when they are pollinated. This allows the backyard gardener the freedom to save his or her own seed from year to year with the assurance that the genetic material in that seed will continue to produce the expected flavor, color, and vigor. If you plant a 'Green Zebra' tomato from seed, harvest the ripe tomato, extract the seeds, dry them, and plant them the next year, you will get a 'Green Zebra' tomato. Over time, the gardener will have selected the plants (and seed) adapted to thriving in the local environment.

Saving seed from open-pollinated plants requires isolating the plants to ensure the variety does not cross-pollinate with another variety growing nearby. Open-pollinated plants are pollinated by wind or insects, or they are self-pollinating, which means cross-pollination with another variety of the same species can occur and intervention is required to ensure a pure seed. Some tomatoes, lettuce, beans, and peas are self-pollinated so the seeds can easily be saved by seed-saving beginners who are not willing to prevent cross-pollination by growing a single variety, isolating the plant, or covering it with a barrier. In general, the self-pollinating vegetables will produce seed that is true to type.

Determinate and indeterminate tomatoes

Determinate tomatoes are small and fairly compact tomato plants, usually growing to heights of less than 4 ft. (1 m). Determinate varieties flower, set all of their fruit at the same time, and then stop growing. This is convenient for gardeners who like to can or cook a large batch of sauce, as all of the tomatoes ripen at the same time. Usually, determinate tomatoes are paste type tomatoes and do not require staking. They do well in containers and in smaller garden spaces.

Indeterminate tomatoes are the vine type tomatoes that continue to branch and grow over a long period of time. They will repeatedly flower and produce tomatoes until they are killed by frost. These plants can sprawl unmanageably as they continue to vine and require staking and pruning for best harvest. Most open-pollinated tomatoes are indeterminate. Planting indeterminate varieties in the potager creates an opportunity for designing beautiful support structures, such as wrought iron cages or painted bamboo poles.

GROWING PLANTS FROM SEED

Although it is always tempting to start seeds indoors too early, as if somehow we can influence the unpredictable spring weather, resist the urge. Plants that are started too early will be leggy as they reach for light, or they may outgrow their containers, making more work for you because you'll need

These calendulas were planted from seed and then thinned; each seedling gets its own square peat pot.

Basil is easy to grow from seed and can be succession planted throughout the season.

to transfer the plants to bigger containers before transplanting them into the garden.

Start by figuring out a safe time to put out the little plants—usually a certain number of days relative to the frost-free date in your area. In central Ohio (Zone 5), after Mother's Day, or the second week of May, is the general marker for when it is safe to plant seedlings into the garden. (Your local extension agent can also help with this.) Use the information provided on the seed packet to determine how long the seed needs to sprout and how many weeks after sowing it takes until it is ready to plant outdoors. Then count back from the transplant date the appropriate number of weeks needed for each variety of vegetable. For example, basil is a warm-season vegetable that is very sensitive to frost. Counting back six weeks from the transplant date in my Midwest garden means I should be starting my basil seeds indoors around March 28 (six weeks before the early May transplant date). Basil plants should be transplanted outside one week after the frost-free date.

You can make your own detailed chart each year in a spreadsheet program (such as Microsoft Excel) that will serve as a record of what you planted when. The accompanying chart (adapted from the *Organic Gardening* magazine website, at http://www.organicgardening.com/) shows an example of such a record. Label the specific variety of each vegetable. Making additional notes at the end of the season will help you remember which varieties worked well in your garden. This becomes your garden journal—a permanent record of your garden that you can reference every year. Though not as romantic as writing with ink in a special leather-bound journal, it is a little more practical. The spreadsheet is easy to share with friends who may be growing a few similar varieties, and they can make additions to the list. These charts are helpful, as crop rotation and seasonal planting plans can make planning large gardens a pretty complex affair.

PLANTING SCHEDULE FOR A ZONE 5 GARDEN

CROP	WHEN TO START INSIDE	WEEKS FROM SOWING	TIME TO SET OUT RELATIVE TO FROST-FREE DATE	SETTING OUT DATE
basil	March 28	6	1 week after	May 16
beets*	March 28	4–6	2 weeks before	April 25
broccoli	March 28	4–6	2 weeks before	April 25
cabbage	March 28	4–6	4 weeks before	April 11
cauliflower	March 28	4–6	2 weeks before	April 25
collards	March 28	4–6	4 weeks before	April 11
corn*	April 11	2–4	0 to 2 weeks after	May 23
cucumber	April 11	3–4	1 to 2 weeks after	May 23
eggplant	March 7	9–10	2 to 3 weeks after	May 23
kale	March 28	4–6	4 weeks before	April 11
kohlrabi*	March 28	4–6	4 weeks before	April 11
lettuce	April 4	4–5	3–4 weeks before	April 11
melons	April 11	3–4	2 weeks after	May 23
mustard*	March 28	4–6	4 weeks before	April 11
okra*	March 28	4–6	2–4 weeks after	May 23
onions	March 14	6–8	4 weeks before	April 11
parsley	March 7	9–10	2–3 weeks before	April 25
peas*	April 11	3–4	6–8 weeks before	April 28
peppers	March 28	6	2 weeks after	May 23
pumpkins	April 11	3–4	2 weeks after	May 23
spinach	March 28	4–6	3–6 weeks before	April 18
squash	April 11	3–4	2 weeks after	May 23
Swiss chard	March 28	4–6	2 weeks before	April 25
tomatoes	March 14	5–8	1–2 weeks after	May 16

* These crops are usually direct-seeded outdoors, but they can be started inside.

A simple setup can be used for growing seedlings under grow lights. Plastic lids keep moisture in until seeds sprout.

Sowing seeds indoors

Although you can grow seedlings in a window that faces south, east, or west, often the plants become spindly and bend as they struggle to reach the sun. Setting up a system of adjustable plant lights is easy and helps the young plants receive the light and warmth they need.

Here's what you'll need:

* Five-tier wire shelf purchased from a hardware store (74 in. high by 18 in. deep by 48 in. wide, though sizes vary)

* Four florescent shop lights, 48 in. (with space for two bulbs)

* Eight plant grow lights (or buy one cool and one warm florescent bulb for the complete light spectrum and rotate your plants daily so each plant receives ample light)

* Eight S hooks

* Wire chain large enough to fit through the S hooks, with eight pieces cut in premeasured lengths to fit the distance between your shelves

* Eight eye bolts with nuts

Here's how you assemble the growing system:

1. Assemble the wire shelf according to the manufacturer's directions. The shop lights will hang off the bottom of shelves, with each shelf holding trays of plants. You can store extra trays or supplies on top of the highest shelf.

2. Remove the metal tops of the florescent light fixtures. In the already existing holes, screw in the eye bolts, one on each side of the lights for hanging. Replace the tops.

3. Attach an S hook to each of the eyes, then a precut length of chain, and then the remaining S hook. The lights can now be hung on each of the wire shelves.

4. The lights should hang about 6 to 8 in. above the seed trays to prevent leggy growth in the seedlings. As the plants grow in height, the lights can be raised by adjusting the chain length.

5. Plug the four cords from the lights into a surge protector with multiple outlets, and then plug this into a timer. You now have a flexible and portable plant light system to grow your choice of specialty flowers and vegetables.

Many home improvement and garden centers sell kits for growing seedlings that contain a plastic bottom container for the seedlings with drainage holes and a clear plastic dome. These can be reused year after year. Before reusing them, thoroughly wash the containers with soap and water; then let them dry out in the sun. I use square peat pots that fit into the plastic growing tray, which saves the step of transplanting the seedlings into a larger container before placing them into the garden, since peat pots can be transplanted directly into the soil.

Fill the peat pots about three-quarters full with a seed-starting mix, which is usually a light soil mix with peat moss and perlite. Place a few seeds on top of the mix in each square and cover them ⅛ in. (3 mm) of soil. Use a system for labeling the planted seeds so you can identify the emerging seedlings. You can use two methods of labeling. One is to write the name of the plant cultivar on a small wooden stick with permanent ink and then place a stick in each square of the peat pot. Another labeling method is to draw a mini-plan of the planting tray on a sheet of paper with the names of the seed cultivars written in each square.

This method is especially convenient if you use peat trays that are divided neatly into 32 compartments. Each row may contain a different variety of eggplant, for example, which you can mark on your plan. Label this drawing and its corresponding planting tray with the same letter or number. The label can simply be ink on a small square of plain paper and attached with tape. When labeling the plastic seed tray, label both the inside tray holding the peat pots and the outside tray that holds the overflow of water with the same label. Label only one side of the tray. This becomes a reference point for the drawing. (The marked side on the trays is the bottom of the drawn plan. Trays can get moved or turned around, so the reference point to the drawing is important.) The plastic tray will have one label such as "Tray 1" or "Tray A." Everything planted in those 32 squares is listed in detail (cultivar name, date planted, and so on) on your plan, which can be kept in a notebook in a convenient, safe place. This method keeps you organized while preventing moldy, lost, or unreadable stick labels. It also becomes a written record of the varieties of seeds grown each year.

Water the seeds with a fine sprinkling and place the clear plastic cover over them; this mini-greenhouse maintains moisture and retains heat. Place the trays under the lights. (Some seeds require darkness for germination; for these, follow the directions on the seed packet.) Set the light timer so the plants receive 12 hours of light per day. The seeds will germinate in a week or so. Remove the cover when the seedlings sprout their first set of leaves to reduce mildew and damping off. Check the seedlings daily and add water as needed. The lights produce heat, so don't allow the soil to dry out.

Thin seedlings with scissors, cutting at the base of each sprout you want to cull. Refrain from pulling out excess seedlings, as it will disturb the tiny roots of the remaining plants. Thin all but one healthy sprout from each pot or square to give this plant room to grow. (Don't fret about killing excess seedlings, as the health of the remaining plant depends on it, and the thinnings can be recycled to the compost bin.) Fertilize seedlings when they have two sets of true leaves.

Setting out plants

Before placing the new plants in the garden, they need to *harden off*, or acclimate to their new outdoor environment. Place the trays and fledgling plants outside for a week and a half or so in a protected area away from wind and full sun. Check them daily to determine if and when they need water. Don't allow the plants to dry out, but also check after a rain to make sure the bottom trays are not filled with water that will drown the roots. If the temperature is expected to drop to near freezing, make sure you bring plants inside or they will be killed.

When the plants have sufficiently hardened off, they can be placed in the garden on a cloudy day or in the evening. Warm-season plants, especially

peppers, tomatoes, okra, eggplant, and basil, need warm soils to thrive, so it's always best to delay planting these crops. Keep a glass cloche on hand to cover these heat-loving plants if necessary.

Dig a hole in the garden bed with a trowel, place the entire peat pot in the hole, and gently arrange the soil around the stem, making sure the new plants' tiny roots aren't disturbed. Tear away any part of the peat pot that sticks out above the soil. Tomatoes should be planted deeper in the ground than they were planted in the peat pots. Tomato stems can actually sprout roots when they're submerged in the soil, and this creates a stronger plant. Don't be afraid to place the plants close together, so that the full-grown plants cover the bed with minimal barren soil between. Vegetables, herbs, and flowers planted densely will crowd out weeds. Tomato plants should be spaced 2 ft. (61 cm) apart. Basil and parsley should be planted 6 in. (15 cm) apart. Leeks, onions, carrots, and beets can be planted every 1 or 2 inches (3 to 5 cm); the row will be thinned as you harvest every other young and tender "baby" plant.

Plants should be hardened off in a protected place outdoors to get used to temperatures and sunlight.

The potager is an ongoing process of planting and harvesting throughout the season. I have just finished covering the poles with twine for the climbing beans. (Photo by John Bartley)

A simple trellis, constructed using bamboo poles, will be covered with rows of twine so that young vines can easily climb.

Much of the spring planting has been done in my potager. As the peonies in the background fade, the yarrow in the foreground will bloom. (Photo by John Bartley)

Direct seeding

Many plants prefer to be sown directly in the garden soil. Such plants include sunflower (*Helianthus*), sweet pea, nasturtium, most beans, cilantro, dill, carrots, corn, peas, radishes, and squash. Basil, lettuce, kale, and kohlrabi can be sown directly in the garden soil or sown inside under lights.

SOIL

The ideal soil for vegetables is dark, crumbly, and rich in organic matter—the kind of dirt in which you can dig a hole with just your hand and feel the moist crumbly particles as they separate in your fingers. Soil that is rich, dark, and fluffy smells good, and the worms like it, too. Unfortunately, most of us start out with soil that is either too sandy or too thick with heavy clay. If the topsoil was scraped off and removed during construction, as is often the case, no soil may be left at all—just a subsoil void of organic matter.

Soil is a combination of mineral and organic materials, water, and air. The mineral component is a mixture of sand, silt, and clay. The amount of each determines the *texture* of the soil, which ranges from sandy to loam to clay. Water and nutrients travel too quickly through sandy soils, so plants languish and dry out quickly. Heavy clay soils retain too much water when it rains, and then they dry to a hard, impenetrable mass. Clay soils lack the necessary air spaces for roots to thrive. Any soil will be improved by

I harvest immature garlic to be used like green onions; the full-grown garlic bulbs will be harvested a month later. Tiny eggplant sprouts were just planted here. (Photo by John Bartley)

The raised bed is ready for planting in the spring; the warm soil is perfect for parsley that will be planted around the edges, as strawberries bloom in the background. (Photo by John Bartley)

As the peonies fade, the parsley continues to fill out. The heirloom tomatoes have been planted and await staking. (Photo by John Bartley)

adding organic material to condition it, bringing it closer to the loamy, well-draining ideal.

Build, enrich, and protect the soil

Building productive soil is a top-down process of regularly adding organic matter and an organic fertilizer to condition the soil and replace depleted nutrients. Nitrogen is lost from the soil as vegetables grow and should be replaced. This can be done by adding at least 2 to 4 in. (5 to 10 cm) of organic matter such as compost, well-rotted manure, or humus every year.

Humus is the dark brown to black partially decomposed plant or animal material that forms the organic portion of soil. It is the by-product of composting. This free additive is an inexpensive way to condition and nourish the soil and one reason composting waste—such as grass, leaves, plant debris, vegetable kitchen scraps, and coffee grounds—is so worthwhile. Find a source for decaying organic material on your own property or from a nearby farm and build a compost pile.

Cover crops and green manures

Soil is a resource to be protected during the winter months when the garden is at rest. When all dead plant debris has been removed from the vegetable garden in the fall, cover the soil with a protective mulch such as straw or plant a winter cover crop, such as rye, annual ryegrass, or crimson clover. These green manures protect the soil from erosion, reduce weeds, and add organic matter back into the soil. Legume cover crops, such as fava beans or winter peas, help to add nitrogen to the spent soil. Cut down the cover crop before it goes to seed and till the cuttings into the soil or remove them to the compost pile.

At the East Side Café in Austin, Texas, the owners create rich compost from leaves from mature live oak trees on the property and scraps from the kitchen. The compost is used to build the soil for the large organic garden that supplies the restaurant with fresh foods.

Lettuce, zucchini, and tomatoes grow in raised beds at the East Side Café; beds are amended regularly with nutritious compost.

PLANTING SPECIFICS: WHEN AND WHAT TO PLANT WHERE

Here are general guidelines for when to plant what based on each particular plant's preference. Some cultivars will extend this limit because of breeding and selection—for example, some types of lettuce will grow in the warm season. Use this information as a starting point when planning your kitchen garden.

Spring (cool-season plants)

beets
broccoli
brussels sprouts
cabbage
carrots
cauliflower
kohlrabi
lettuce
onions
parsnips
peas
radishes
scallions
spinach
turnips

Summer (warm-season plants)

basil
beans
corn
cucumbers
eggplant
melons
peppers
pumpkin
squash
tomatoes

Fall (cool-season plants)

beets
broccoli
cabbage
carrots
endive
kohlrabi
lettuce
radishes
spinach
turnips

FAST FILLERS

These vegetables and greens are fast crops that can be grown as part of a multiseason plan or can be used to fill holes in the potager quickly when other crops have been harvested.

arugula	lettuce
baby beets	mustards
baby carrots	purslane
cresses	radishes
dwarf peas	rapini (broccoli raab)
endive	spinach
green onions	turnips
kohlrabi	

SHADE-TOLERANT PLANTS

These plants will tolerate some shade conditions.

Vegetables

arugula	malabar spinach
beets	mallow
burdock	mizuna
cabbage	mustard greens
carrots	nettles
celery (leaf)	New Zealand spinach
chicory	pak choi
Chinese cabbage	perpetual beets
collards	radishes
cornsalad (mâche)	sorrel
cresses	spinach
endive	Swiss chard
escarole	turnips
fennel	
garland chrysanthemum	**Herbs**
Jerusalem artichoke	angelica (alexanders)
kale	anise hyssop
kohlrabi	borage
leeks	chervil
lettuce	chives
	ginger

goldenseal
hyssop
lovage
lemon balm
marjoram
mints
parsley
perilla
rosemary
salad burnet
savory (summer and winter)
tarragon
thyme

Fruits

blueberry
currant
elderberry
paw paw
rhubarb
serviceberry
strawberry

Edible flowers

calendula
Johnny-jump-ups
nasturtium
pansies
sunflower
violets

SEED AND FRUIT SOURCES

Baker Creek Heirloom Seeds
2278 Baker Creek Road
Mansfield, MO 65704
Phone: 417-924-8917
Fax: 417-924-8887
www.rareseeds.com

Bountiful Gardens
18001 Shafer Ranch Road
Willits, CA 95490-9626
Phone: 707-459-6410
Fax: 707-459-1925
www.bountifulgardens.org

W. Atlee Burpee & Co.
300 Park Avenue
Warminster, PA 18974
Phone: 800-888-1447
Fax: 800-487-5530
www.burpee.com

The Cook's Garden
P.O. Box 1889
Southampton, PA 18966-0895
Phone: 800-457-9703
www.cooksgarden.com

Eastern Native Seed Conservancy
P.O. Box 451
Great Barrington, MA 01230
Phone: 413-229-8316
www.enscseeds.org

Fedco Seeds
P.O. Box 520
Waterville, ME 04903
Phone: 207-873-7333
www.fedcoseeds.com

Harvest Moon Farms and Seed
Company
P.O. Box 143
Union City, IN 47390
Phone: 765-964-3971
www.felcopruners.net

Johnny's Selected Seeds
955 Benton Ave.
Winslow, ME 04901
Phone: 207-861-3900
www.johnnyseeds.com

Nichols Garden Nursery
1190 Old Salem Road NE
Albany, OR 97321-4580
Phone: 800-422-3985
Fax: 800-231-5306
www.nicholsgardennursery.com

Raintree Nursery
391 Butts Road
Morton, WA 98356
Phone: 360-496-6400
Fax: 888-770-8358
www.raintreenursery.com

Renee's Garden Seeds
7389 W. Zayante Road
Felton, CA 95018
Phone: 888-880-7228
www.reneesgarden.com

John Scheepers Kitchen
Garden Seeds
23 Tulip Drive
P.O. Box 638
Bantam, CT 06750
Phone: 860-567-6086
Fax: 860-567-5323
www.kitchengardenseeds.com

Seed Savers Exchange
3094 North Winn Road
Decorah, IA 52101
Phone: 563-382-5990
Fax: 563-382-5872
www.seedsavers.org

Seeds of Change
Phone: 888-762-7333
www.seedsofchange.com

Seeds West Garden Seeds
317 14th Street NW
Albuquerque, NM 87104
Phone: 505-843-9713
www.seedswestgardenseeds.com

Territorial Seed Company
P.O. Box 158
Cottage Grove, OR 97424-0061
Phone: 541-942-9547
Fax: 888-657-3131
www.territorial-seed.com

Thompson & Morgan
P.O. Box 1308
Jackson, NJ 08527-0308
Phone: 800-274-7333
Fax: 888-466-4769
www.seeds.thompson-morgan.com

Trees of Antiquity
Phone or fax: 805-467-9909 or
805-467-2509
www.TreesofAntiquity.com

GARDENS OPEN TO THE PUBLIC

~~~~~~

Call each garden for open hours.

Antique Rose Emporium
10,000 Hwy 50
Brenham, TX 77833
Phone: 800-441-0002 or 979-836-5548
Fax: 979-836-7236
www.antiqueroseemporium.com

Château Saint-Jean de Beauregard
91940 Saint Jean de Beauregard
France
Phone: 33 (0)1 60 12 00 01
Fax: 33 (0)1 60 12 56 31
www.domsaintjeanbeauregard.com

Château de Villandry
37510 Villandry
France
Phone: 33 (0) 2 47 50 02 09
Fax: 33 (0) 2 47 50 12 85
www.chateauvillandry.com

Ferme Médiévale de Bois Richeux
28130 Pierres Maintenon
France
Phone: 33 (0)6 11 88 20 20
Fax: 33 (0)1 46 24 56 00
www.boisricheux.com

Le Potager du Roi
10 rue du Maréchal Joffre
78009 Versailles
France
Phone: 33 (0)1 39 24 62 62
Fax: 33 (0)1 39 24 62 01
www.potager-du-roi.fr

Le Prieuré d'Orsan
18170 Maisonnais
France
Phone: 33 (0)2 48 56 27 50
Fax: 33 (0)2 48 56 39 64
www.relaischateaux.com/en/search-book/hotel-restaurant/prieureorsan/

North Hill
Readsboro, VT
Open to the public on selected days in June, July, and August to benefit AIDS Project of Southern Vermont
Phone: 802-254-8263
Fax: 802-254-3613
www.AidsProjectSouthernVermont.org

Chef's Garden
Dragonfly Neo-V Cuisine
247 King Avenue
Columbus, OH 43201
www.dragonflyneov.com/

East Side Café
2113 Manor Road
Austin, TX 78722

The Ryland Inn
Route 22 West
Whitehouse, NJ 08888
www.rylandinn.com/garden.htm

BIBLIOGRAPHY

Aben, Rob, and Saskia de Wit. 1999. *The Enclosed Garden: History and Development of the* Hortus Conclusus *and its Reintroduction into the Present-day Urban Landscape*. Rotterdam, Netherlands: 010 Publishers.

Anthony, Diana. 1998. *The Ornamental Vegetable Garden*. Toronto, Ontario: Warwick Publishing.

Antoine, Èlisabeth. 2000. *The Medieval Garden*. Paris: Musée National du Moyen Âge.

Barash, Cathy Wilkinson. 1998. *Kitchen Gardens: How to Create a Beautiful and Functional Culinary Garden*. New York: Houghton Mifflin.

Bird, Richard. 2000. *The Kitchen Garden*. New York: Stewart, Tabori & Chang.

de Bonnefons, Nicolas. 1658. *Le Jardiner François*. London: John Crooke.

Booth, Norman, and James Hiss. 2002. *Residential Landscape Architecture: Design Process for the Private Residence*. Upper Saddle River, NJ: Prentice Hall.

Bowe, Patrick. 1996. *The Complete Kitchen Garden: The Art of Designing and Planting an Edible Garden*. New York: Macmillan.

Brennan, Georgeanne. 1998. *In the French Kitchen Garden: The Joys of Cultivating a Potager*. San Francisco: Chronicle Books.

Brennan, Georgeanne, and John Vaughan. 1998. *Potager: Fresh Garden Cooking in the French Style*. San Francisco: Chronicle Books.

Carvallo, R. 1991. *The Gardens of Villandry: Techniques and Plants*. Joue-les-Tours, France: R. Carvallo.

Chamblas-Ploton, Mic. 2000. *Jardins Médiévaux*. Paris: La Maison Rustique, Flammarion.

Clarke, Ethne. 1987. *The Art of the Kitchen Garden*. New York: Alfred A. Knopf, Inc.

Clevely, Andy. *The Kitchen Garden: A Practical Guide to Planning & Planting*. New York: Sterling Publishing.

Coleman, Eliot. 1989. *The New Organic Grower*. White River, Vermont: Chelsea Green.

Comito, Terry. 1978. *The Idea of the Garden in the Renaissance*. New Brunswick, New Jersey: Rutgers University Press.

Creasy, Rosalind. 1986. *The Gardener's Handbook of Edible Plants*. San Francisco: Sierra Club Books.

———. 1999. *The Edible French Garden*. Boston: Periplus Editions Ltd.

Crisp, Sir Frank. 1924. *Mediaeval Gardens*. New York: Hacker Art Books.

Cutler, Karen Davis, ed. 1997. *Tantalizing Tomatoes*. New York: Brooklyn Botanic Garden.

Eck, Joe, and Wayne Winterrowd. 1995. *A Year at North Hill*. New York: Little, Brown and Company.

———. 1999. *Living Seasonally: The Kitchen garden and the Table at North Hill*. New York: Henry Holt and Company.

Ford, Peter. 2001. In busy Paris, a quiet garden of medieval delights. *Christian Science Monitor* (2 January).

Gertley, Jan, and Michael. 1999. *The Art of the Kitchen Garden*. Newtown, Connecticut: The Taunton Press.

Hales, Michael. 2000. *Monastic Gardens*. New York: Stewart, Tabori & Chang.

Harvey, John. 1981. *Mediaeval Gardens*. Portland, Oregon: Timber Press.

Hill, Thomas. 1987. *The Gardener's Labyrinth: The First English Gardening Book*. Based on 1652 edition. Oxford, U.K.: Oxford University Press.

Jeavons, John. 1974. *How to Grow More Vegetables than You Ever Thought Possible on Less Land than You Can Imagine*. Berkeley, California: Ten Speed Press.

Jones, Louisa. 1995. *The Art of French Vegetable Gardening*. New York: Artisan.

———. 1997. *Kitchen Gardens of France*. London: Thames and Hudson.

———. 2000. *The French Country Garden: Where the Past Flourishes in the Present*. New York: Bulfinch Press.

Kelley, Mary Palmer. 1983. *The Early English Kitchen Garden: Medieval Period to 1800 AD*. Columbia, South Carolina: Garden History Associates.

Kummer, Corby. 2002. *The Pleasures of Slow Food: Celebrating Authentic Traditions, Flavors, and Recipes*. San Francisco: Chronicle Books.

Landsberg, Sylvia. 1996. *The Medieval Garden*. London: Thames and Hudson.

Lesot, Sonia. 2000. *Au Temps des Jardins Medievaux, Les Saisons au Prieuré d'Orsan*. Paris: Editions du Garde-Temps.

Lesot, Sonia, and Patrice Taravella. 1997. *Les Jardins du Prieuré Notre-Dame d'Orsan: A la Recherché d'un Jardin Medieval*. Arles, France: Actes Sud.

MacDougall, Elizabeth B., ed. 1986. *Medieval Gardens: Dumbarton Oaks Colloquium on the History of Landscape Architecture* 9th ed. Washington D.C.: Dumberton Oaks Research Library and Collection.

McClure, Susan. 1997. *Culinary Gardens: From Design to Palate*. Golden, Colorado: Fulcrum Publishing.

Messervy, Julie Moir. 1995. *The Inward Garden: Creating A Place of Beauty and Meaning*. Boston: Little, Brown.

Ogden, Shepherd. 1992. *Step by Step Organic Vegetable Gardening*. New York: Harper Collins.

Pereire, Anita. 1999. *Gardens for the 21st Century*. London: Aurum Press Ltd.

Phillips, Roger, and Martyn Rix. 1998. *Salad Plants and How to Grow Them*. New York: Random House.

Simonds, John O. 1998. *Landscape Architecture: A Manual of Site Planning and Design* 3rd ed. New York: McGraw-Hill.

Stewart, Martha. 1991. *Martha Stewart's Gardening Month by Month*. New York: Clarkson Potter Publishers.

Stokstad, Marilyn, and Jerry Stannard. 1983. *Gardens of the Middle Ages*. Lawrence, Kansas: Spencer Museum of Art.

Taravella, Patrice, and Sonia Lesot. 1997. *The Gardens of the Prieuré Notre Dame D'Orsan*. Arles, France: Actes Sud.

Thompson, Sylvia. 1995. *The Kitchen Garden: A Passionate Gardener's Comprehensive Guide to Growing Good Things to Eat*. New York: Bantam Books.

Turner, Carol, ed. 1998. *Kitchen Gardens: Beyond the Vegetable Patch*. New York: The Brooklyn Botanic Garden.

Waters, Alice. 1996. *Chez Panisse Vegetables*. San Francisco: HarperCollins Publishers.

———. 2002. *Chez Panisse Fruit*. San Francisco: HarperCollins Publishers.

Weaver, William Woys. 1997. *Heirloom Vegetable Gardening: A Master Gardener's Guide to Planting, Seed Saving, and Cultural History*. New York: Henry Holt and Company.

Wells, Patricia. 1996. *Patricia Wells at Home in Provence: Recipes Inspired by Her Farmhouse in France*. New York: Scribner.

Wetherall, Megan. 2000. Fruits of Her Labor. *Garden Design* 19 (4): 86–95.

Wilson, C. Anne. 1998. *The Country House Kitchen Garden 1600–1950*. Gloucestershire, U.K.: Sutton Publishing.